American Schools
The $100 Billion Challenge

Dwight Allen, Ed.D.
and
William H. Cosby, Jr., Ed.D.

iPUBLISH.com
at Time Warner Books

Ⓦ A Time Warner Company

ISBN 0-7595-5000-X

First edition: October 2000

Visit our Web site at www.iPublish.com

Dedication

To all those who want to join in the quest for dot-com leadership in education, whether as leaders or supporters. They are the hidden treasures of the future of American education.

And to Ennis Cosby, who was on his way to becoming a dot-com leader in education, particularly in his chosen field of special education. He never got that chance. But in a very real sense he is responsible for this book: he brought us together at this transformational time, the stimulus for us to join forces to call for the transformation of education in America. His spirit is with us all, assisting in this unprecedented effort.

—*Dwight Allen and William H. Cosby, Jr.*

Contents

Needed: Dot-com leadership for education.

Wanted? Not yet.

That's why we wrote this book.

We need a whole new concept of educational leadership: young (and young in spirit), vigorous leaders who are encouraged to take risks and are given the resources and support to respond to new challenges as they emerge. One of the biggest problems in American education today is "safe" leadership. Educational leaders come from ranks of teachers schooled in obsolete teaching practices, conditioned by bureaucracy to "fit in," and often indebted to the forces of nepotism, politics, and political correctness.

These leadership criteria are fatally flawed in times of rapid change. The leadership pool of educators is already weaker than we would like—witness all the complaints about mediocre teaching. It is amazing that we have as many dedicated, effective leaders as we do, given the selection bias, lack of incentives, and limited talent pool. The crisis in educational leadership has given rise to suggestions as wild as scrapping public education entirely—to create a free-market system built around private (even for-profit) schools. Home schooling is another desperate response for those fortunate few who can even consider it.

Public education can and must do better. Before we consider a "new school system," let us find new leadership. First of all, we must encourage these leaders to take risks, because the largest risk of all is maintaining the status quo. Second, we should develop new participatory leadership patterns that involve teachers, students, and parents, and seek active community support. Current patterns of leadership have produced isolation and distrust among these groups.

Education needs dot-com leaders desperately. Dot-com leadership for education is the educational equivalent of the dot-com leadership in the business community, which has transformed not only commerce and industry but the basic fabric of America. The stereotype is that they are young, and most of them are likely to be, but dot-com leadership is a state of mind, not an age. Nor is dot-com leadership tied to any particular training—even training in technology, its progenitor. Dot-com leadership implies vision, risk-taking, caring, sharing, and enormous energy. Our colleague, Patrick O'Shea, who is just finishing his doctoral study at Old Dominion University and who helped us with research on this book, is an excellent example of an emerging dot-com leader in education.

Dot-com leadership can take shape by establishing the National Experimental School Administration (NESA) laid out in this proposal. Such a system would give America a laboratory in which to test and evaluate educational reforms and can become a clearinghouse for our knowledge about educational practice. NESA schools would become frontiers for educational change.

The challenge will be to open up the system—not an easy task. But it starts with a vision of change, a vision of new potentials, with mechanisms that allow local communities to try them out.

The $100 Billion Challenge for American Education

We are asking America to invest $100 billion a year to transform our schools. One hundred billion dollars is $400 per year for every American. It's a significant amount of money to spend, but we can't afford not to spend it. Moreover, in a period of unparalleled prosperity, it is unacceptable that the wealthiest nation on earth is failing to educate 20 to 30 percent of its children.

The cold war is over. The immediate crisis is past. Yet we still spend $265 billion annually on our federal defense budget, more than $1,000 per year for every American, compared to $43 billion a year on education. The discrepancy is ironic, because education is also a matter of national security. The future of America rests on a well-educated citizenry, and we are increasingly recognizing that our security is jeopardized by school systems that fail to keep up with our national needs.

We are willing to spend more than $10 billion on a single hurricane. When a hurricane hits, FEMA, the Federal Emergency Management Administration, literally comes to the rescue. FEMA doesn't take over; it provides support.

Sometimes a hurricane will highlight other problems—and as a result, new regulations and safety measures are drafted. It's the hurricane that redefines the needs, not FEMA. Similarly, the Federal Aviation Administration creates the rules for air safety and develops common markings for runways and regulations for managing air traffic. It doesn't build and manage the airports it supervises, but we rely on the FAA for our safety—knowing that it doesn't perform perfectly. There simply isn't an alternative.

The federal government needs to help with education—not take it over, but help. And that help must be massive to make a dent in the challenge we face. Transformation of education won't be cheap, and it won't be without mistakes. Those mistakes will be costly, but we can and will learn from them. It will require courage and commitment. Waiting will only make problems worse—more costly and more traumatic. Each generation of students we sacrifice to obsolete, ineffective education will cost us financial and social capital, and increased resources will be needed to protect society from the consequences of our hesitation—more welfare, more prisons, more alienation and conflict.

Our challenge is to create a new and appropriate federal role for education in the new millennium. And while our politicians are talking about up to $800 billion in *tax cuts*, we'll tell you what we can achieve if we have the courage to invest $100 billion a year in our country's educational future. What we are proposing is a bold, unprecedented journey to redefine education, its structure, its goals, and its staff. It will be a journey as long and as necessarily uncertain and transformative as the process of electrifying

America was a century ago. We can open up entire new vistas of human potential. We can create a workforce capable of developing not only powerful new inventions but also the skills to use them.

The private sector and particularly the dot-com leaders need to rethink how they can engage American schools in new ways—from providing systematic discounts to teachers for goods and services to providing systematic "pro-bono" support for schools. They can help build bridges between schools and communities through such initiatives as instituting personnel policies that make it possible for their employees to volunteer in the schools on company time and receive office phone calls from teachers.

The first half of this book explores the issues and challenges education faces; the second half details what we believe are real-life solutions, including a bit-by-bit plan for how to allocate $100 billion. At the heart of our proposal is the establishment of a National Experimental School Administration, a nationally administered educational laboratory that would allow us to test and evaluate the widespread reforms our nation so clearly requires. We hope that *American Schools* will, at the very least, provide a starting point for a discussion of education: more important than any specific proposal is the idea that education requires a complete rethinking—and at a national level.

We have new tools that can transform the process of education itself. We need to understand these tools and their potential, to experiment with their use, and to integrate them into our system. We have new, competing needs and opportunities in society, and we can't afford to have these opportunities compromised, by either neglect or obsolete responses. We have new criteria for success and failure—in the workplace, in families, and in society as a whole. Education is the key for our success individually and collectively, and our current patterns are woefully inadequate, built on premises that are no longer true. In these dynamic times of change—which will only accelerate in the new millennium, we must build a new educational system that expects to constantly upgrade its response, one that has the ability to transform itself.

PART 1
Educational Reform: A Status Report— Needs and Responses

Control and Decision Making: A Balance of Local and National Control

To argue whether education is a national, state, or local responsibility is to miss the point, because by necessity it is all three. Decisions must be made at all levels in an interdependent society. We do have common skills, experiences, and needs that are national in scope. We must acknowledge the need for both local and national coordination and regulation. We cannot let a local community choose to have bad schools or be trapped into bad schools by ignorance or circumstance.

On the other hand, we must allow for local creativity and the design of programs to meet unique local needs. Both good schools and bad schools affect everyone, everywhere. Families move, students study in public and private universities outside their home states, industries recruit nationally for a constantly evolving labor market; in short, the movement and consumption of goods and services do not follow local or state boundaries.

We need unity and a national consensus. We must assert

minimum standards, minimum shared objectives, and clearly understood elements of achievement for our educational system. We must clarify these common standards and make sure that they become the starting points of effective education and not the end of our efforts. We urge local communities to be creative and add to these standards. Communities must give their schools individual identities, exploit resources, strive to offer higher standards of excellence, but a strong, national core must be present without apology. The economies of scale become very important in an electronic age where the high "up front" costs of lessons and materials become reasonable only with wide application. It is foolish for each teacher to generate an individual lesson plan for every lesson. Yet it is equally essential for teachers to have the right, and the time, and the resources to generate their own powerful, local lessons to use and share with others. Individual teachers will have more time to make unique curriculum contributions if they have the maximum help and support of common materials for agreed-upon national curriculum modules.

The time has come to reexamine our entire system of public schooling and, through our efforts to do so, define new relationships between federal, state, and local governments. Note that nowhere in this book do we propose national control of education. Instead, we seek a balance. We realize that there are educational concerns best addressed at the state and local levels, but we argue that there are needs, opportunities, and solutions that are national in scope and, thus, require national solutions. We don't know—and indeed, it is impossible to predict—where our suggested initiatives would lead us nationally. This should not be a point of apprehension; rather, we should be excited about embarking on a journey that has the potential to open new frontiers of understanding and suggest alternatives we might never have considered.

In 1969 we went to the moon, uncertain what we would find. We were only confident that we would benefit from finding out. To illustrate our point, we ask the question: How can anyone *not* be excited by the possibility of an America in which every child has a computer and knows how to use it, every teacher has training in curriculum and methods, and the profession of teaching attracts and holds top university graduates? Although we are unsure what objections might be raised through efforts to answer that question, we *are* sure that right now, none of these things is true. Education is stalled in its present configuration and is trapped into obsolete patterns of teacher training, time schedules, organizational patterns, curriculum, and funding. Now is the time to free ourselves from these constraints. We have the resources as a nation to fund any new educational initiative we choose. All we need is courage and the kind of commitment we made when as a nation we decided to put a man on the moon.

Change

Change is an increasing component of our lives, and it is often immobilizing. The complexities of our new world are too new to be comfortable. It may seem unfair that just when you reach the zenith of your profession, the world changes and makes many of your skills obsolete. Your expertise becomes a hurdle to overcome as you struggle to see the brave new world.

Fifty years ago, the government issued a report that calculated the total potential world market for computers—for the entire planet—at fourteen. Now we live in a world where, likely, there are more than fourteen computers in your family car. It's logical that such a pace of change will turn education upside down. It also is inevitable that we will struggle through trial and error to find the best responses. Change, however, can be a powerful ally.

Let's look at some guiding principles:

1. The pace of change will accelerate. There will be more change and these changes will be unpredictable.
2. The rate of knowledge production will also accelerate.
3. Knowledge and expertise will become obsolete quickly.
4. Society will be more mobile and interdependent, making new levels of coordination vital.
5. Individuals will change careers many times in a lifetime. Even in the same career, the knowledge requirements will change dramatically.
6. Teachers will often learn along with their students.
7. Knowing where to find knowledge will be more important than the acquisition of knowledge.
8. The process of learning will become more important than the content of learning.

Change Is a Necessary Consequence of Scientific Discovery

We have to understand more fully the world being created by scientific inquiry, but where to begin? Little in life occurs in a linear fashion, which means that there is rarely a clear-cut "starting point." This list represents a small sample of issues that affect us simultaneously:

1. Transportation and communication have completely redefined the boundaries of time and space.
2. The sophisticated harvesting of natural resources has created the potential for wealth unimaginable to the economists of even a century ago.
3. The sophistication of weapons of mass destruction has made us realize that no one wins a war. Now any war raises the specter of unimaginable horror.
4. The interactions between races and cultures are redefining cultural and traditional boundaries.
5. The recognition of women and men as equals is beginning to redefine the relationships of family and society.
6. Virtually unlimited access to information transforms the goals of education.

With such changes swirling around us, education must be geared to respond to new information, new processes, new complexities, and new relationships. We can no longer afford the luxury of an educational system that no one shapes or guides. We must develop new mechanisms for dis-

17

cussion and decision making about the process, the content, and the structure of education. Systematic experimentation must be a part of that process. The expectation of flux and change must be a part of that process. We must replace our expectation of stability in education with the expectation of change, and then become willing to invest resources to shape such changes.

Space Exploration: A Model for Long-Term Change

America's pursuit of space exploration demonstrates what is possible with long-term national commitment. Although our national space program has had many ups and downs, for the most part, NASA has used its mistakes as learning tools. For example, the Hubble Telescope had a faulty lens and was criticized as a waste of money and resources. With perseverance, however, it has become a magnificent instrument of learning. The nuclear-powered Cassini probe, which cost $3.5 billion, is as complex and costly as it is controversial. It took a long time to decide what the satellite would do, but now it's on its way to Saturn. If we are patient, Cassini will provide results—even if they are not the results we expect. It may not arrive at the ringed planet, but its launch still constitutes a step in the right direction. The cost of experimentation cannot be measured by dollars alone.

Our efforts to reach the moon have yielded unexpected benefits, from ceramic stovetops to the global positioning systems. We take for granted that we can get television from around the world because of geo-stable satellites that the space program put in place. Of course, there have been risks, costs, failures, and disagreements, but space exploration continues to transform the potential of civilization because we have focused on the impact of our successes rather than on the failures.

If we maintain a similar attitude about education, we could explore the learning space just inside the classroom door.

Our Multicultural World

The world we inhabit is diverse in ways unimaginable even a generation ago. When we get the weather on television it is the weather of the whole nation, not just our locality. When air turbulence tosses a giant airliner around over the Pacific Ocean, it is news in Pittsburgh and Paris. We worry about bird flu in Hong Kong and we are more likely to know that Elizabeth is the queen of England than to know the name of the mayor of a town a few miles away. It takes only days for a new hit song to be heard in remote villages in Africa. Barbie dolls are made in China, and McDonald's makes more money overseas than in the United States. There is now a focus on interdependence and global reality.

Unfortunately, in our schools children are more likely to be learning about a world that no longer exists. Knowledge is power; ignorance is oppression. We are oppressed if we don't know, understand, and appreciate our neighbors around the world. We need this knowledge to understand why they act the way they do, what they believe in, and what they consider to be important.

For example, within thirty years of reestablishing our contacts with China, we find our world transformed by that economic relationship alone. The nature of this relationship is hotly debated: China is too powerful a nation for us to discontinue our dealings with its government, but our understanding of Chinese motivations and values is woefully lacking. As China assumes its rightful position as a leader on the world stage, its society will be transformed, and so will ours. We will obviously be better off if we can learn to work together without fear. We can avoid arms buildups, which are enormous drains on all national economies.

How do we begin, though? First, by learning that the "American way" is not *the* way but *a* way of doing, thinking, celebrating, or learning something. And often it's not even the best way.

The manner in which we study other cultures is also very important. When Dwight Allen was in the fourth grade, he studied houses around the world. His project was to build a Filipino house out of toothpicks. This was just one of many "funny houses" that he learned about. The lesson was about how exotic other houses were, and not too subtly, how lucky we were to live in our fine American homes. The teacher never told the class that those peculiar structures demonstrated excellent problem-solving skills: that building a house on stilts in a steamy forest keeps the dampness out, gives small jungle creatures less access, and provides better ventilation. Clearly, simply studying cultures is not enough. Kids must appreciate those cultures. Teachers must become the translators of cultural differences. A child from any nation in the world may be in their classroom tomorrow, and different cultures are just down the street. We need to teach our children to celebrate diversity and the creative human spirit.

How foolish to offend someone because your decisions are based on bad assumptions.

World View of Change

The more insight we gain into our heritage, the more we realize we must look beyond the Western world. We must gain understanding of some of the less studied issues in history; such as the contributions of women, the impact of Islam on the evolution of Europe, the movement of knowledge from East to West via the early explorers, the likelihood of common human ancestors for us all. African and Asian archeological digs deepen our understanding of who we are and where we came from, perhaps more so than European and American excavations. They show us how our roots extend to Northern Africa, Asia, and the Middle East. We now understand that both Islam and Christianity grew from the same religious heritage and have more similarities than differences.

We must be open to learning new ways of understanding how we relate to each other. This requires that we realize the history of the entire world is relevant to understanding our past and, vitally, our future. Although this new awareness is flooding our consciousness, it is difficult to accept because it challenges our most deeply cherished traditions—including those involving teaching and learning. We see ourselves as a Western Civilization, not as a part of the global human family. We don't recognize the influence of the Muslim civilizations that came to Europe through Spain. The Chinese had an age of exploration a century before Columbus's voyages—and their ships were wider than the Santa Maria was long. We remain ignorant of so many of the high civilizations of the past. That doesn't serve us well in the age of global unity. We envy the discipline of Chinese students, but fail to study elements of their culture and traditions that might translate into better discipline for our American kids. We need an entirely new attitude toward the world.

Reform: Why We Need It!

Perhaps these four character studies provide the best introduction to a section on why reform is necessary.

Mitch

Mitch needs help. He's seventeen, and his life has been a disaster until now. For two years he didn't have a place to live. His mother is a crack addict. He's done lots of things he's not proud of. For a year, he was in jail for an uncontrollable temper—not juvenile home—jail. But now Mitch is ready to transform his life. He wants to get away from his old street friends. He knows that he needs an education, and wants to go to college. But the schools don't want him. He's too high a risk, and though he hasn't gotten into trouble at school, the school authorities found it convenient to shuffle him off to the alternative school—that way he won't bring down the test scores, which are the new preoccupation of American education. Mitch is at least two years behind in school. Although he is very bright and a quick learner, the alternative school is overcrowded and understaffed. He'd like five courses, but they gave him only three—just enough to count him for state funding. His English class has forty-five students, and the last session was canceled because the teacher was briefing a police officer about the assault he'd suffered at the hands of a student earlier in the day. His algebra class has only eight students; most students in the alternative school aren't ready for algebra. Mitch, however, has already passed algebra, but he's repeating it because it's the only math class available. His third class is a consumer skills course. It won't count for college, but it was available, and Mitch enrolled late. Welcome to the underworld of education—the part we don't like to think about or talk about.

Kids like Mitch need more resources and more help if they are to have any chance. To be fair to the school district, most of the kids at the alternative school aren't ready for transformation, and the school has become callous—it has effectively given up trying to help them. The resources simply aren't there. With the exception of the occasional teacher still consumed by the desire to help these forgotten kids, most of the staff has given up, too. Eventually we'll pay the price in welfare, prisons, and beefed-up law enforcement. More likely than not, we'll blame the kids for not learning, and then we'll blame the welfare mothers and the prison alumni for not making their lives work, even though they have few skills to work with.

Dale

Dale is a more inspiring subject. One of the lowest-paid superintendents of schools in one of the poorest school districts in the state, Dale recently turned down a private-sector job paying five times his current salary. He loves what he does, and he does it well. The school district doesn't deserve to have Dale, but he's a local boy and is trying to transform his community. The statistics are all against him—25 percent of the adults in the county have a ninth-grade education or less. Almost 90 percent of his students are eligible for the federal free lunch program. Dale is an educational technology buff and has managed to put together grants and temporary funding to make his school district one of the most technologically advanced in the state. He believes that properly used, technology can help turn education around in his county and transform the community. His teachers are poorly paid, and his senior staff stays only because of his personal example of devotion. All have been offered better-paying jobs elsewhere. His vocational students assemble the computers as part of their training. Dale's schools are making giant strides and delivering an awesome performance. But their achievements are built on sand. If Dale leaves, it will be almost impossible to find someone to carry on his work. The schools he leaves behind will go back to being at the bottom, as expected.

Susan

Susan is a fourth-year teacher in an inner-city school. She loves teaching, and she loves her kids—even the difficult ones. She coordinates the school's technology program. She has already been offered many higher-paying jobs in the private sector, but so far has resisted them because of her devotion to her craft. Susan has been "promoted" by the principal of the school to teach only upper-level math classes—the ones that are the most fun for teachers—as a way to keep her. Of course, that leaves her less capable colleagues with bottom-level classes filled with unmotivated kids. But it's triage at work—and Susan is too valuable to lose if she can be enticed to stay. It's getting harder each year.

George

In 1989, George was President of the United States. He wanted to be remembered as the education president. He called the first National Education Summit, and all the governors came. They pumped up the rhetoric, even coming up with national goals: The United States would be first in the world in science education by the year 2000. The media had been publishing reports about how little geography American kids knew, so the governors decided to break apart the social studies curriculum and have separate national goals for history and geography.

It's now ten years later. George meant well. He is no longer president, and we are still complaining about how American kids don't know about geography, science, and math compared to kids in other industrial nations. Our lofty aspirations to lead the world in science by 2000 have been abandoned. It is 2000. And geography never became a separate school subject. We haven't been willing, as a nation, to make the necessary investment in education. Yet we continue talk a lot about educational reform.

The Nature of Reform: Scientific Method

Reform comes slowly and can be made only when the traditional way of doing something is proved inefficient or ineffective. We must continue to challenge age-old "theories." The scientific method is a process in which attempts to disprove a hypothesis are made through testing and experimentation. Once a hypothesis has survived repeated tests, sometimes spanning several lifetimes, people forget it is only a theory and accept it—incorrectly—as fact. This is the problem with prevailing educational methods: People have forgotten that they are based on theory. As a result, educators and administrators are reluctant to challenge established theory and practice. Experimental school districts would enable us to gain new perspectives on traditional methods as well as sites to test various new reform theories. With systematic investigation into current practice, new alternatives can be better shaped and tested. Long-term, experimental schools will provide us with the opportunity for effective educational research.

Educational Research

The article, "The Social Consequences of Bad Research" (Kappan, Jan. 1998), contends that "researchers" often have axes to grind; thus their results are suspect. Tobacco companies had "research" findings that cigarettes were not addictive. Reading specialists have "research" findings both for and against the teaching of phonics. It is true that the methods of scientific research are evolutionary and developmental, and it is difficult to know how much attention to pay to any one "research" finding. Not surprisingly, often the evidence of multiple studies is confusing. This is particularly true in education, where it is much harder to assemble unambiguous evidence for any specific educational practice, and the interactive effects of many variables make it difficult to identify "best practice." As a result, teachers and administrators will blithely ignore research that does not meet their intuitive criteria.

We must get our act together concerning educational research. Not only do we need better research about teaching kids to read, we need help to evaluate and use it appropriately. We need more opportunities to try out all research findings in many different school settings over significant periods of time. Then we can systematically revise and update our educational practices as we gain experience.

The Dangers of Accepting Judgments of Educational Success

There is temptation to reduce all judgments to numbers or simple comparisons. We want to know which program or student is "best," most often without regard for the criteria used. In truth, how "the best" is defined and found depends a great deal on who is looking and how they are looking. There are many "bests" along different dimensions. When we gain an awareness of the futility of determining any one "best," then we gain a greater understanding of what it will take to succeed. Some educational criteria can and should be measured, but many important educational variables cannot be measured precisely. Service programs, extracurricular activities, or programs that promote aesthetic awareness and the creation of a more beautiful community are examples of programs that are difficult to evaluate with objective measures. Instead, we collect subjective judgments and convert them to numbers that can in turn be tabulated. We should not fool ourselves into thinking that such tabulations can constitute objective measures.

These measures are approximate, sometimes fleeting, and perhaps even misleading. Schools need to be places to experiment and test ideas. They must have the latitude to make mistakes, while still remaining accountable. In the absence of certainty, choices still must be made. Simultaneous educational reform strategies should be used. In some cases, parallel programs can be offered in the same school, giving students choices as to which alternative to pursue. Over time we can gain experience with both alternatives and continue to refine and develop them. With funding for research and systematic study of the alternatives, we can gain more confidence in our choices. However, it shouldn't end there. Since we can never be sure that current choices are even likely to be the best alternatives, we must have designated schools systematically developing new alternatives for consideration.

Using Without Abusing Contradictory Findings

It becomes very difficult to know how to respond to research findings when they are contradictory or apply to specific populations and circumstances. This is one of the problems of social science research. In the fine print, researchers state that their findings apply only to the population studied. This is quite proper because there are dangers in generalizing the findings to other settings, but rarely do we have the opportunity to replicate the research in systematic ways.

With decisions to be made, someone must judge whether the available research evidence justifies adopting, continuing, expanding, modifying, or discarding the program under study. A good example is the requirement of summer school. The idea is solid. The implementation has had mixed success. There is a big difference between "summer school" as an add-on, and year-round schools, but they tend to be lumped together in our minds. It's so very hard to distinguish between a bad implementation of a good idea and a bad educational practice. Researchers are aware of this problem, and they have tried to develop techniques to allow the comparisons of findings across studies. This is difficult since protocols and analytical processes are different in every study. The time has come for us to realize the severity of this problem and to develop predictable ways of responding. Our proposal for the establishment of a national experimental school system goes a long way toward solving this problem.

The Ability to Validate Findings

One of the strengths of the American system is its openness. You can find a school to try almost anything, but somehow we have to find mechanisms to survey the options, trends, and results so that we can make judgments concerning what works and why.

A literature is emerging about "learning organizations." These are organizations that have the ability to learn from experience. Learning organizations empower their employees to offer suggestions and challenge current practice. They are organizations that are willing to take risks to try new approaches and ideas. They are organizations willing to stay with a new approach that doesn't immediately bear fruit to see if it has the potential to become successful. We desperately need large-scale efforts to create and evaluate learning organizations in education. This is why we advocate the establishment of an experimental school system national in scope with resources to test alternatives using widely diverse populations and circumstances. We propose to establish two independent, parallel governing bodies for this system, and divide the experimental schools into at least two groups to provide perspective. They will cooperate and share, at the same time mounting and testing their own initiatives. We will see what works best and have systematic alternatives for comparison. Even this process will sometimes produce inappropriate responses. This is inevitable; we don't know enough to be "right" every time. Society is better served by the judgments of impartial observers acting in its behalf, though, than by media hype and lobbying efforts.

It is a travesty when the amount of publicity given to a program relates more to public relations than to educational substance. For example, five years ago Dwight Allen was working with the Norfolk Public Schools in the PRIME program—with innovative teacher internships, new protocols for professional appraisal, and opportunities for innovative staff development. At the very same time that preliminary evaluation results validated the experimental initiatives, politics at Old Dominion University led to the cancellation of the program.

In a society where everyone has the right to express views, however unpopular, we need to figure out how to protect experimental initiatives until we can get a real sense of how they're working. Somehow we must find a way to keep the views of a privileged, vocal few from determining educational policy. This problem is not limited to the world of education. It is a widely held view, for example, that in America we get as much justice as we pay for, but it is vital to find the relative truth of competing theories. An educated public is the guarantor of a more just government.

Fads and Trends

Fads are irresistible in times of change. When we are frustrated by what isn't working, we resort to "faddish" behavior. As frustration builds, a new idea emerges. This idea is sometimes research-based, sometimes the result of media frenzy, and sometimes simply the by-product of exaggerated hope. It becomes fashionable to adopt this "fad." Several times in the past century we abandoned a narrow focus on academics to acknowledge a concern about the "whole child," only to swing "back to the basics," and then to the whole child again. Both positions were inappropriately exaggerated.

The power of the media has grown in the past fifty years. It wasn't too long ago that the whistle-stop was the favored way for politicians to get access to people, but a thirty-second commercial can reach 100 million people now. The mention of a product on television can shape its success or failure. Vivid pictures of a DC-10 crash following on the heels of other incidents with the same plane model generated so much fear in the public that airlines stopped purchasing that particular aircraft. Later it was found that the airframe was not to blame at all; instead, the crash was a result of faulty maintenance. Yet the DC 10 has yet to shake its bad reputation.

In the same way, the media have created an impression of failing public schools. Teachers have to read media accounts that cite illiteracy rates as high as 30 percent of the population and other stories about teachers reading at barely eighth-grade level. Such reports are simply not credible; they erode public confidence in education and make it even more difficult for teachers to function. Although public schools are struggling, they are not failing. Schools all over the world have problems, such as the need to be reconceptualized in the face of obsolescence, but it is not correct to say our schools are worse off than others. It is almost impossible to make accurate comparisons, because each country defines its goals differently—even though every nation is under pressure to be better than all the others. True, significant populations of American kids are not well served, but the uninformed comparisons made by the media leave a false—and harmful—impression. Kids from more affluent families are taken out of the public schools, further weakening their base of support and leaving behind a disproportionately difficult population of kids to teach.

With a loss of confidence comes more pressure for external testing and accountability. We don't trust the schools to police themselves. Standards are important, appropriate, and necessary. But many of the accountability initiatives today are ill conceived, misleading, and counterproductive. They tend to force teachers to focus on skills that are easily counted and detailed rather than on the more important but difficult-to-test thinking skills, like creativity and character development.

What Is School Reform?

Schools are obsolete by any reasonable standard. The school day and school year were defined to meet the needs of an agricultural society. We are no longer a "Western civilization"; we are a world civilization. Many kids and teachers are succeeding in spite of the system rather than because of it.

It's one thing to know that we need to change, but it's quite another to build a consensus of what to do and how to do it. There are more issues than can be counted. A small sample of the problems to be faced includes:

- finding the right balance of local, state, and national control
- outdated or inadequate classroom technology

- lack of equipment
- inadequate facilities
- unmanageable class size
- teacher selection
- education and professional service
- school schedules
- curriculum revision
- improving school safety
- student and teacher diversity
- family instability
- moral erosion
- ignorance
- prejudice
- waste
- the sources and amounts of funding

Piecemeal Reform

We have had endless reform without changing much. Although our reforms have been thoughtful and well done—we've developed new, more rigorous science curricula and found ways to help students become more active learners—there are so many factors involved that it is almost impossible to find causal relationships between our efforts with individual reforms and the "big picture" success of students. With more than 15,000 school districts in the United States, it is nearly impossible to get any consensus. It's one thing to copy a successful individual practice from another district, but it's something quite different to free our schools from obsolescence and outdated governance structures.

34

Even reforms that have been judged successful have trouble gaining national adoption. The Head Start program is perhaps the best example. In the 1960s it was demonstrated to be one of the most cost-effective ways to head off educational disaster for a substantial number of kids. Thirty years later, after lots of political rhetoric and recommitment to its cause, we still haven't fully funded the program to reach its target population. We must do better.

One of the urgent problems we face as a society is that one third of America's young African-American males are involved in the justice system in one way or another. Their lives aren't working. Many of them have been unsuccessful in school. They, along with all the kids who are unsuccessful in school, are threats to the tranquillity of our society. It requires a solution more creative than longer jail terms and larger prisons. Minorities are certainly not the only ones having problems with the schooling they encounter. It is just that, as a group, they have fewer personal resources to fall back on when the system does not work.

Only when school reform systematically addresses the real, embedded problems of education and provides resources both to pursue bold alternatives and to examine, evaluate, test, and implement the results, will we make significant progress. Until then, all our reform efforts add up to little more than the illusion of change.

Mobility

Americans like mobility. We expect to move around from one area of the country to another. Yet even as we change jobs and neighborhoods, we like predictability—whether it is the taste of our hamburgers, the style of our favorite music station, or the availability of our favorite talk show. The same can be said for schools. We like our schools to be similar enough that our kids aren't hurt by a move. Unfortunately, with local control being the objective of every school district, this cannot be the case.

It's ironic that although our universities are national, recruiting students from across the country, our individual school districts yearn to be local. The result is that 15,000 individual districts are all expected to prepare students for all 3,000 of our colleges and universities. In essence, we have, confusingly enough, standardized our lack of standardization.

Thus far, we have not been asking the right questions or pursuing the right strategies to allow significant reform. For example, everyone agrees that reading is important, but there are dozens of ways to teach reading. All of them have advantages and disadvantages. At the moment, the way a kid learns to read depends on what side of the road he lives. In one school district they might teach phonics, while in the school district across the street they might use the whole language approach. The former teaches kids to sound out words; the latter assumes that students will learn the specific structures of language by using them in context. Over the past decades education has swung wildly from method to method with great acrimony.

We are buried under research on reading. The question we have been unable to answer is: Who can we trust to sort it all out? We don't know enough to say precisely how each kid will best learn, but we do know that some approaches work better than others, and that some practices are perpetuated only through the dead hand of tradition. Extremes of any kind will leave some kids out. Not surprisingly, a new consensus is emerging, albeit too slowly and painfully, that early phonics followed by whole language learning is most often successful.

Ambiguity of Goals

We live in a diverse society with many individual goals and aspirations. This multiplicity is one of the greatest assets of American society; however, there are common goals and values that are necessary to its success as well. Such values as honesty, justice, trust, generosity, fairness, dependability, and honor are all a fundamental part of the American way. As society becomes more complex and diverse, we must develop the mechanisms to agree on the boundaries of common values and build a social fabric flexible enough to support agreed-upon differences.

Once the goals of education are articulated, educators can and should be charged with fulfilling them. While vigorous debate demonstrates the health of a democratic society, schools must have confidence to know what they are being asked to teach. That our values will continue to change should be expected and encouraged. We as educators must develop the means to acknowledge and respond to these changes.

DWIGHT ALLEN, ED.D., AND WILLIAM H. COSBY, JR., ED.D.

The Curriculum: Introductory Issues

There is growing sentiment that we need to develop and test experimental national curriculum elements. The controversy over how to teach reading illustrates just how badly educational research and development are needed. As part of our commitment, we call for the development of new curricula to systematically test educational theory for as long as it takes to get good evidence. With enough funding, multiple curriculum programs could be developed and tested simultaneously. Constant curriculum development, testing, and revision should become a natural part of educational practice.

New curricula are needed to incorporate new neurological research that targets learning. Current brain research strongly suggests that the most creative scientists have extensive exposure to the arts. And brain research confirms many new ingredients in the learning process itself, including neurological principles to guide both learners and teachers. All students and teachers would be well served to have a course or courses on both new psychological and neurological learning principles included in the curriculum. There is no shortage of other candidates for curricular attention: the environment, global studies, health and nutrition, and the arts, to name just a few. But, as a nation, we are immobilized to even begin on substantial, systematic curricular reform.

We have had many national curriculum efforts in the past, the best known being the National Defense Education Act (NDEA) which was created in response to the *Sputnik* scare. In 1957, the USSR succeeded in placing the first man-made satellite, a beeping object about the size of a large grapefruit, into orbit around earth. In and of itself, *Sputnik* was not extraordinary. You must remember, however, that in the mid-1950s America was in the middle of the Communist scare, and nearly everyone took this launching as a sign that not only was the USSR's space program superior to ours, but they were also on the verge of invading the United States In response, the American government started the NDEA. With a focus on math and science education, this would eventually lead us to the moon. Many of the reforms funded by NDEA have had lasting effect, and others proved ineffective, but there was never a systematic way to test them over time or to compare results. And there was no funding to develop other initiatives based on NDEA curricular successes.

Typically, funding was for three- to five-year cycles, for both development and implementation. Little or no funding was available to investigate the impacts of experimentation. Too often programs were abandoned as priorities or politics changed before conclusive results were obtained. We've had "new math," team teaching, flexible scheduling, transdisciplinary curriculum, and writing across the curriculum, all of which have had some success but have never made it into the mainstream of American education. There is some merit to all, but even now, more systematic implementation and evaluation are needed.

Basic Skills

What should kids learn? What do they really need to know to function successfully in society today, and more important, what will they need to succeed in the world tomorrow? Clearly, more skills are needed than simple reading, writing, and arithmetic—though those durable basics are still important. But they must be joined by other basics, equally important in an increasingly complex society.

Many efforts have been made to redefine the basics. One that we particularly find useful is the SCANS report, a summary of which is found in the second part of this book.

There are lots of very strongly held opinions, and there are many traditions to guide and misguide us. Educators, prodded by persistent problems in the system, become blinded by enthusiasm and wind up chasing rainbows in order to find their pot of gold: knowledge. In the last century, knowledge has exploded, there are rainbows everywhere, and no one can chase them all. It is obvious that basic skills must make kids both smart and good, and we have new awareness that everyone must have a stake in the new world order for it to be successful.

Learning and Thinking Skills

One of the objectives of education is to teach thinking skills. This will require a system in which the teacher is held responsible for the learning of each class, within a broad framework of common curriculum goals.

We need teachers who are trained to learn from their

students. For this to occur, they must be alive intellectually, and constantly updating their skills. We will have to provide systematic opportunities for lifelong learning for teachers as a part of their profession. Later we will detail our specific proposal to reach every teacher in America with regular in-service training. We need teachers who will teach their students to share new information. Together they must be prepared to evaluate the credibility of this information and to process it in relation to other sources. There are near-universal recommendations for student involvement in the learning process, such as peer editing of writing, but how much should students be involved in defining their own learning process?

This debate has raged back and forth for almost a century. Obviously, students learn more when they have a part in defining what and how they will learn, but allowing students to participate often leads to confusion, especially when teachers are not prepared to respond to agendas they do not propose and control. Sometimes it will be impossible to know in advance what will be learned, and there will be disappointments. Effective teachers, however, can help students learn from these mistakes. Although these options are new, well defined, and tested, they are implemented inconsistently. And some are controversial. This is why teachers must have a clear mandate of what is expected from society. But whence will they obtain this mandate? We believe that our proposed National Experimental Schools Administration will provide a starting point.

Brain research shows that active learning is much more powerful than passive learning, but this will require redefinition of the teaching process. As of now, project activities, activities that incorporate real-world experiences into learning, are seen as "too slow." It is true that in project learning, teachers have less control over what is learned, and less material can be "covered," but this means that teachers need to be skilled enough to respond. In project learning, teachers are asked to make judgments about which questions to pay attention to, when to investigate an unexpected topic, when to follow up an issue in depth, and how much controversy to expose. A higher level of professional expertise will be needed, and we must develop a corps of master teachers—another of the proposals we will detail.

Controversy can be a powerful teaching tool. Presently, we often adopt convenient deceits in our curriculum. Students are not typically taught about how the "West was won" by a succession of deceitful "treaties" with the Indians, which promised lands that were later confiscated as we discovered new uses for them.

A second example involves the arbitrary rules of the English language. Students are taught the "right way," the "correct spelling," and that essays require "the five-paragraph plan," but there's a difference between teaching students that arbitrary patterns are "the right way," and the practical fact that standard conventions are needed to facilitate communication. Students should be taught that although there are guidelines to writing, these "rules" are far from absolute, and many of our most brilliant writers flouted them. The same is true for mathematics—there may be multiple solutions for a given problem.

Character Education

As we've said, the two most important reasons for education are to make kids smart and to make them good. By raising smart kids without concern for their moral education, we unleash a danger on society. To avoid this, we need to study the history of education.

The first legislation in the United States requiring the establishment of public schools was entitled "Ye Olde Deluder Satan Act." This created, in Massachusetts, the first public schools for the purpose of keeping kids from Satan's clutches. Back in 1647, people believed that children who lacked a proper education could be too easily influenced by the devil. Unreal and unreasonable as this sounds, it is, at heart, true. Without a proper education, one that teaches children to understand our responsibilities to others, they may develop truly evil practices. There are too many examples, from six-year-old murderers to sixty-year-old welfare cheats, for us not to face the reality that improperly educated kids can be evil. Though some might say it is simply human nature to cheat, lie, and steal, we disagree. From reformed murderers to recovering alcoholics, there is abundant evidence that people respond to a higher sense of dignity and worth. There is a constant tension between what we as a society really would like to do—our vision—and what we are able to achieve, given all our weaknesses. Proper education helps us realize more of our higher aspirations. It gives us hope, and if it is based in real-world examples, it shows us what can be done and how we can see ourselves as a part of the prosperity of all humankind.

We are both thinking and feeling beings. Education must attend to both aspects of ourselves. We must develop a conscience that requires us to act according to what is "right." But what is "right"? There are many definitions of right and wrong in our society. There is room for different values and beliefs, but we also share values and beliefs in common, starting with our laws. This is a good starting point for education. We must teach respect for the law. Right now in America respect for the law is in danger. Some smart kids are starting to believe that only suckers obey laws, and some smart adults are becoming increasingly cynical about the respect for the law shown by their leaders. Our education should condition us to make sound moral judgments and to be offended by immoral actions by anyone, young or old, high or low, rich or poor.

The family is the starting point for character education. There is no substitute for the family when teaching values, and only a foolish society would try to undermine family's role. But why is it so frowned upon to also teach values in school? The main reason is that many people have difficulty trusting the schools to teach their core values. Yet we agree on most of the values in our society: basic values like truth, honesty, integrity, respect, courtesy, generosity, justice, and cleanliness. If families can get together with schools to teach these fundamental ideas, these concepts will surely sink in.

A multitude of surveys confirms that trust is one of the core values of our society. Without trust, the society cannot function, families cannot function, and schools cannot function. We are all immobilized by a lack of trust. Trust itself is not controversial, though there is despair about whether we can achieve it. How silly that trust is one thing we are trying to teach, but we don't trust ourselves, or others, to teach it!

Let's commit ourselves to teaching the values we agree on. And let us decide what to do about values we don't agree on and commit ourselves to find ways to deal with these disagreements rather than let them block the effective education of our children. For example, most Americans believe that God—or at least some concept of the Divine—should have a place in school, while a vocal minority find this a gross violation of the separation between church and state. We have to find ways to honor the rights of minorities without allowing them to impose their views on the majority.

Much work must be done. The best way to teach values is to demonstrate them. Right now, schools don't do a good job of modeling values. Teachers and administrators often make no secret of the fact they don't trust each other. In addition, grown-ups in general, including teachers and school administrators, don't often act like they trust kids. In some cases, it's because teachers don't know enough to be fair. Homework can be late because of a genuine emergency, but it's hard for teachers to know whether the emergency is real or an excuse. Adults won't guess right all the time, but if kids believe they are trying to be fair and just, it makes a difference.

Waste in Education

There is much waste in education, some of it because we misuse our resources, some of it because we don't know enough to select our alternatives well and avoid waste, and some because we don't have enough resources. Furthermore, waste is very hard to define. For some, arts and extracurricular activities constitute a waste. Others, including the authors of this book, disagree. We believe developing the arts is a vital and neglected part of a truly successful society. Brain research confirms the synergism between artistic and technical thinking, but that has not stopped schools from slashing their arts programs.

Is it a waste to create an aesthetic environment for teaching and learning? In one local school district in Virginia, a multimillion-dollar bond issue for rehabilitating the schools was defeated because one new school had been constructed with a $40,000 flagpole. Though the flagpole might have been extravagant, there was no need to punish every child in the district.

A scandal in the Defense Department has demonstrated that entrenched bureaucracies are often rife with waste. How can we really be sure we no longer have $750 coffeepots in military passenger jets? But did we insist that waste be eliminated from the military before we *increased* our peacetime military expenditures? Of course not. The government deemed national defense too vital to slash its budgets. Although we must take pains to avoid this sort of mismanagement, so too must we realize that some waste, misdirection, and mistakes are inevitable in reforming education. The trick will be differentiating good mistakes from bad mistakes, timely mistakes from untimely ones, and preventable mistakes from inevitable failures. It is by risking mistakes, and suffering the consequences, that we learn to distinguish these differences. How sad it is that in most schools, teachers are more concerned about preventing all mistakes than about giving kids the chance to make them in a safe environment where the consequences can be controlled.

After all, any child who does not achieve the necessary skills is at risk—at risk to commit crimes, to become a welfare charge, to act irresponsibly. This is the most terrible waste of all, and the cost to society is very high. Negative behavior costs our society enormous sums of money, to say nothing of the fear and lack of tranquillity that result when our streets are unsafe. There is no excuse for poverty in the richest nation in the world.

The question we should ask ourselves is: Can we afford to withhold needed funds for crucial personnel, equipment, buildings, and repairs just because there is waste in the system? Can we as a society afford to compromise the education of a large percentage of our youth (most of them poor) just because our system is flawed? The simple truth is that effective education has to become a higher priority in society—whatever the cost.

Although rarely cited, one of the largest educational wastes springs from our decentralized system. Because curricula are unpredictable from district to district, and because an average of 20 percent of students move every year, teachers must spend up to six weeks each year reviewing material in order to get new arrivals and continuing students "on the same page." This means that since we cannot agree on a common national curriculum, we waste up to one sixth of available instruction time. That's certainly more waste than almost any other example mentioned. It's not just 15 percent of teachers' time, but also salaries and the total cost of schooling.

Beloved as they are, summer breaks are also wasteful, both in terms of lost instruction time and the skills and knowledge that children forget. Even the structure of the school day is wasteful. In the days when most women were stay-at-home moms, it made sense to dismiss kids in the afternoon. But now, when most children come from homes where both parents work, it makes little sense to send kids home to empty houses or to expensive—and often less than satisfactory—child care.

It is also wasteful to force well-trained professionals to moonlight in order to make ends meet. Many teachers work in low-level service occupations to supplement their salaries. We want our teachers to be professional, yet we aren't offended when they serve as cashiers in convenience stores, even though we would be shocked to find our cardiologist working a register.

Other perceptions of waste are simply inaccurate. Teachers are often thought of as part-time employees due to short school days. Some people argue that it would be wasteful to pay teachers competitive professional salaries when their service is limited in this way. There are documented studies, however, that show that teachers typically spend in excess of fifty hours a week on school-related tasks. Rarely do teachers go home empty-handed. With papers to grade, lessons to plan, parents to call, school plays to direct, and PTA meetings to attend, they are just too busy. Plus, teachers are expected to upgrade their skills in the summer, most often at their own expense.

Leaving Bad Teachers in the Classroom Is a Waste

There are some bad teachers. This is a fact that cannot be disputed. The number of really incompetent or misbehaving teachers is not large, probably no more than 5 percent. But that percentage is extremely destructive. Not only do they hurt the kids, but they also poison the public image of teaching and ruin public support for the large numbers of dedicated, underpaid, and overworked teachers who prop up a bad system.

What can we do about it? Three approaches are possible. First, we can wring our hands and complain, as we do now. Second, we can try to change the tenure rules and get rid of the bad teachers, a task that even the most optimistic anti-bureaucrat won't find easy. Third, we can systematically provide support for the bad teachers to give them the opportunity and the incentives to perform better. That's not easy, either, and it will be expensive.

We propose to provide additional, intensive training for weak teachers and to differentiate responsibilities so that weak teachers are under the supervision of their more skilled colleagues. This would create a situation in which a teacher works with a staff. A staff would provide teachers with technical and clerical support, more eyes and ears to respond to individual needs, and help in developing lessons and working with the community. Such an innovation would require both substantial expenditure and substantial research efforts to develop new strategies and new professional roles.

Since we've never mounted a massive, systematic professional development program, we'd have to try out different approaches and evaluate their success. Some of these approaches will fail and be wasteful, but the process is far more desirable than to go on doing nothing about our worst teachers. Investing in the better performance of teachers and developing new professional incentives are a vital part of eliminating waste in education.

It Is Wasteful to Train Teachers Poorly

We continue to complain about the quality of our teachers, but we have neither invested the resources to train them well nor provided the professional opportunities that would attract top-notch candidates. Teachers have only one third the professional training of lawyers and less than 20 percent that of doctors. We doubt anyone seriously believes that teaching is the easier profession.

The fact that teacher training is relatively brief is an outmoded and unfortunate legacy of the nineteenth century. Because teaching was dominated by women, and women were expected to get married, have children, and then stop teaching, it didn't make sense to spend much time or money on their training. Since then, the roles and responsibilities of teachers have changed dramatically, but training patterns have largely remained the same. Teacher training consists of about three years of general education and teaching specialization and one year of pedagogical training. Recently we have patched on a bit of technology training and tried to beef up the amount of practical experience required, but teachers still arrive in the classroom fully certified and wholly untested in terms of real-world performance. Although teachers will always need to complete in-service training, especially as the pace of change continues to accelerate, we must begin by training teachers well. In addition, we must commit ourselves to advancement protocols that are equivalent to other professions. If we fail to do this, our best-trained teachers will leave.

Over-Administration

Our educational systems, particularly the largest ones, are overburdened with a surfeit of administrators. Every dollar spent on administration takes a dollar away from the delivery of services to kids. No doubt some of those administrative dollars are necessary, even well spent, but in too many instances, these large bureaucracies are created because we don't trust our teachers. Therefore, we must invest money auditing, monitoring, and reviewing, all of which is as expensive as it is endless.

Administrators, curriculum specialists, area supervisors, deans and vice principals in charge of discipline, department heads, and staff development specialists are all there to support teachers. At present, teachers need this kind of support because they are weak. They are weak because they have minimal training and the profession is not "senior" enough to attract the best and the brightest.

It's a vicious cycle: teachers are weak, so they need support; support is costly so less funding is available to pay teachers; strong teachers leave for better-paying opportunities, weak teachers who need more support are left. Ironically, the greatest erosion of teacher talent comes from promotion to better-paying administrative positions. With each new administrative function we create, such as grant writing, public relations, accounting, and medication dispensing, we take resources away from teachers. We must experiment with different alternatives and at least staff the bureaucracies in part with persons who have no teaching background. Although it will be costly to do, it will be worth it when we can be confident about the results.

In addition to creating large bureaucracies, we manifest our lack of confidence in our teachers by placing ever-greater emphasis on external testing. Apparently, we can't count on each other to be honest in either our dealings or our evaluations. Ironically, as recent scandals demonstrate, the increased emphasis on external testing increases the motivation for teachers to "cheat" and help their students on tests.

The endless organizational reform of education is wasteful, but this is not to say that reform is not needed. Every year, a new reform is adopted. Whether site-based management, teacher quality circles, or block scheduling, we move from one reform to another, never pausing to learn which ones work. We simply don't have the patience or the resources to find out. A reform may fail because it is genuinely ineffective, or it may fail for political reasons, or because we lose interest, or because it cannot be carried out in isolation. Some reforms fail simply because funding runs out. Thus far, we have had little way of knowing. We propose to select reforms carefully, test them extensively over time and in different settings, provide support and encouragement, and provide resources for their further revision and development.

Problems and Opportunities: The Problems

Our schools need access to every kind of technology, from the Internet and PowerPoint to computer-generated images and self-instruction materials. Most schools now haven't even got the budget to buy an initial round of technology. Take, for example, Ruffner Middle School. It is the technology showcase of Norfolk, Virginia's, public school system. When it opened, it was state-of-the-art. The problem was that the teachers knew how to use only about 10 percent of the new equipment. The other 90 percent just collected dust.

Teachers, administrators, and supervisors worked hard to learn to use the new computer software, accommodate the automated administrative procedures, and help students to direct their own learning. Understandably, this took a while. Unfortunately, the technology was outdated almost before everyone learned to use it. The Norfolk public schools had an ugly choice. They could either upgrade the technology again in the same middle school, or they could put a first round of technology in one of the other schools. Which choice is better: Let the model school become obsolete, or bring another school on-line?

The choice Norfolk made was to upgrade the technology of Ruffner. In our opinion, this was the better choice because it helped us learn all that is required to keep schools up-to-date with technology. After making the investment in technology, we must spend an additional 20 to 30 percent of that original expenditure every year just to keep the technology current. Experimental schools must show the way. Fifty-five other Norfolk schools are waiting to enter the age of technology. But even as the expenditure for technology increases, Norfolk is falling further and further behind.

Costs and Opportunities

We need to reform the way we fund education. We continue to rely on property taxes for educational dollars, even as we know that income from property tax is seldom equitably distributed in relation to real education need. In the past twenty-five years some progress has been made at the state level—recognition that local property taxes are a very regressive way to fund schools. For instance, the tax base generated by a given business may not be in the school district where its employees live. Often a poor area will tax itself at a high rate only to produce less revenue than the neighboring, affluent school district with much lower taxes.

These divisions are unacceptable. We all benefit from well-educated kids. We all suffer from the effects of inadequate education. We must find new ways to fund schools more equitably. A national funding base would be an obvious answer, but at the moment it is politically remote as a possibility. Our $100 billion educational initiative provides an attainable, intermediate step. As you'll read, we offer a few key initiatives that we hope will excite the nation and begin the process of true educational reform.

Ideally, the funding for society's basic needs should come from general revenues, but recently we have found it more attractive to fund educational initiatives from special sources like lotteries and user taxes. A hundred billion dollars is a lot of money, but education is the foundation of national security. After all, we wouldn't pay for aircraft carriers with a tax on soda pop.

Dissemination of Knowledge

The dissemination of knowledge seems so straightforward. You study a problem, try different approaches, discover the best course of action, replicate it to verify that it works, then disseminate it so others may share the benefits. This way, we all "improve" our practice.

We have federally established national dissemination networks, such as regional educational laboratories to facilitate this process, but they barely scratch the surface of what is needed. The answer to this problem isn't simple, because the problem isn't simple. We live in a society that celebrates diverse elements. Local variety is almost as popular as the trendy "first on the block" syndrome. Either element is amusing when it comes to cars or designer style, but it's deadly serious when the matter concerns education.

We haven't learned how to validate educational practices and determine the circumstances under which they are effective. We can't decide how to disseminate new knowledge, and we haven't accepted the responsibility of providing the resources to disseminate effective new practices to those most in need. One thing is clear: the neediest schools have the fewest resources.

Priorities and Resources

So many things cry out for attention in education. We know that poorly educated kids are almost certain to become criminals or require welfare. We must do more for children with special needs. Teachers aren't trained to know how to respond to some of the most common health problems such as asthma or attention deficit hyperactivity disorder (ADHD).

We lament the boredom of gifted children and wring our hands when we can't respond to new curriculum demands. Meanwhile, our teachers have become obsolete in their skills and knowledge. New teachers are trained with outdated knowledge and methods, even though brain research demonstrates the need for new approaches to the educational process. Brain research tells us that a joyful classroom is conducive to much greater learning. Brain research tells us that applied knowledge is remembered longer than isolated facts. Brain research even tells us that our brains need mental exercise to develop properly. We need to further investigate how the principles of brain research can be translated into practice.

We are confounded by the demands of local and national priorities. We must find ways to overcome the gridlock that keeps principles of moral and character education from being effective components of schooling. The list of needs is endless, but the resources are not. Priorities are unclear, and, worse, we can't understand how to address priorities effectively as a nation.

We need both governing and regulatory bodies that inspire our confidence, from local school boards to state legislatures. If we can have confidence in the competence of the people guiding the decision making, all but the most skeptical observers will be relieved.

Revision and Redirection of Institutions and Practices

It is appropriate for educational decisions to be made to respond to the specific needs of society at local, state, and national levels, but we must find ways to get systematic examination. Competition in the private sector produces decisions. These are not always the best decisions—the technically superior Sony Betamax lost out to the VHS format for videotape simply because of marketing pressures—but they are definitive. Some education reformers advocate grafting a market model onto education in order to let competition provide perspective, including the establishment of for-profit schools, but competition doesn't provide incentive for many of the important decisions that are necessary. Competition has a role, but service is much more important as a motivator.

The Crucial Role of Evaluation

In general terms, evaluation is the source of most personal and societal improvement. The most common evaluation is informal, but there are limits to the value of intuitive experience. Logic and evidence are important sources of progress and change, but not all change will be logical. It shouldn't be. Any time we get systematic evidence, we increase the likelihood of making good decisions. We must ask for evidence, evaluate its credibility, and use it in our decision-making process. We desperately need to apply this process to education.

It seems more important for the teacher to know everything about a subject than to know how to convey the knowledge effectively. This simply isn't true. Effective teachers must have skill in the teaching process. This is not to say that methods are enough, but that instead, knowledge is not enough. We live in times when knowledge is constantly changing. Teachers must help their students evaluate knowledge and realize when to skip anything they "know." The content of learning must be seen as a series of examples to build on, not a storehouse to be shared.

Building a National Consensus

One of the great things about American society is its ability to transform itself rapidly. Americans pride themselves on having the "latest" model everything. Of course, sometimes the newest is not the best. We pay a high price for going in many directions at once. In general, though, being pioneers is to our advantage. We must find ways to use this to transform our schools.

There's a paradox here. Having a decentralized school system allows "a thousand flowers to bloom," but this makes it difficult to get the full benefit once we learn something. There are very important educational options that can't be done piecemeal, but to make them possible we all have to agree.

This goes back to trust. Whom do we trust to make decisions about our schools? Failing education is in the headlines constantly. We have demonstrated that almost all kids can learn if they have the right school. But the system hasn't been able to deliver. Someone must step up and be trusted to make informed choices for our schools, our children, and our country.

How can we build a national consensus about education? How can 250 million citizens agree on anything so complex? There will always be differences of opinion, but we can generate a sense of fairness if ordinary citizens believe that their voices will be heard. The first task is to appoint a national school board to oversee the experimental schools—we'll discuss this in more detail later. If the experimental board works well, we hope it will pave the way for the appointment of a board to oversee all of American education, a board charged with the responsibility to protect the balance of local regional and national control.

It is time for us to provide the resources to ready the nation for the continued hurricanes of change in education. It's time to spend $100 billion a year of our national financial treasure to protect the future of our greatest national treasure—our children.

Long-Term Effects

The most important effects of education are long term. Although a student may successfully solve a problem on a test, if a week later she forgets how to do it, that would not be successful education. Yet the overwhelming evidence shows that our standard processes of accountability—tests, along with the methods of education leading to them—put overwhelming emphasis on the short-term recall of information. This is further exacerbated by the new insistence on "narrow accountability" which requires teachers to teach for the test. New evidence from brain research demonstrates that learning in context is much longer lasting than knowledge gained through isolated study. The problem of measuring the effects of education months or years after instruction is daunting, and if we are to do this successfully, we must provide resources for long-term and large-scale experiments. We also must give priority to the development of divergent instructional practices that have potential for achieving desired outcomes. Finally, we must have the will and provide the resources to implement the results.

Love the Kids

Look at successful teachers. They love kids! It is almost impossible to really be successful in the process of education if you don't enjoy what you are doing. We now have the evidence of brain research to show that happy brains learn and teach better. Joy is an energizer.

One of the greatest challenges of education today is to institutionalize joy. The way it happens now is almost accidental. Many teachers bring joy to their classroom in spite of the system rather than because of it. Teachers are always fighting off distractions and roadblocks. Ironically the current "standards" movement in education forces teachers to be narrowly concerned about individual bits of knowledge. We have to make joy a priority and provide teachers with an appropriate scope of tasks that provide both time and incentives for bringing joy to the classroom.

It's not hard to see how joy gets lost in schools. In part it comes from thinking that joy dilutes or subverts rigorous learning, whereas the opposite is true.

Joy and love are prerequisites for effective learning. They are not learning objectives. That's a distinction that must be made. It's foolish to think that all we have to do is make kids happy and they will learn. Let's be very clear—a happy, secure, loving environment makes learning possible. Without these factors, learning becomes very difficult, and for some, impossible. The only practical way to think about joyful learning is to focus on the total learning environment. Joy is the prerequisite, not the goal of learning. When joy is present in a learning environment, it becomes easier to teach whatever the agenda of learning is, with even more rigor than is possible without joy.

Joyful learning requires everything from joyful, competent, confident, and secure teachers to school leaders who reward teachers. Joyful learning requires students who are unified and focused on learning and are rewarded for creating a cooperative learning environment. Their parents will know the schools, communicate with the teachers, and provide support for school at home. Joyful learning takes place in communities that provide attractive, well-equipped, and well-maintained school facilities with strong community support.

The Power Pyramid

Increasingly, we have to face the reality all around us that the world is changing. And the pace of change is increasing. Everywhere we can see signs of new levels of cooperation and involvement as new solutions emerge for old problems, and old solutions are discarded.

War, as a form of decision making, is becoming obsolete. It is increasingly evident that everyone loses a war. The world is struggling to find alternative means for conflict resolution.

As we realize that some strategies produce no winners, we look for new methods. Sometimes we simply need to develop a new level of awareness of changes that have already taken place.

Let us examine two models that illustrate our changing human potential, this new level of civilization, which is already within our grasp, a perspective on prosperity that makes peace inevitable.

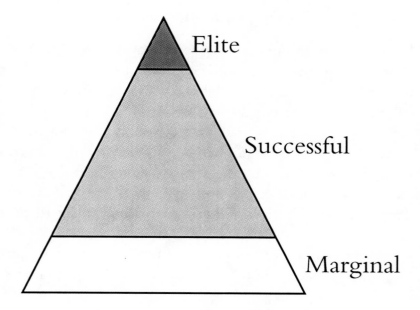

Elite

Successful

Marginal

Social Strata in a Static Power Structure

The Pyramid of Privilege and Power

There are many ways to think about the structure of society. A common image is that of a pyramid, where privilege and power are concentrated at the top. This image is reinforced by the reality that absolute equality is impossible. But we have still not accepted the fact that absolute equality is undesirable. Equity should be the objective, not equality. Equity relates to fairness, not sameness. There is often confusion in the way the words are used, but the strength of America is in its quest for fairness—the equitable sense of equality.

Power in a Static Society

Power is concentrated at the top. Those of us fortunate enough to be at the top of the pyramid of power, to be honest, do not want our children to be deprived of the same power we have had—and we aspire for them to have more. So any social change that threatens those of us in power will have to be stopped somehow. We will employ whatever excuse or subterfuge necessary to make our self-serving strategies seem consistent with the values of democracy: the illusion of equal access, and power to the people.

Fortunately, we live in an ever-advancing civilization, and the world is changing (in fact has already changed) to make

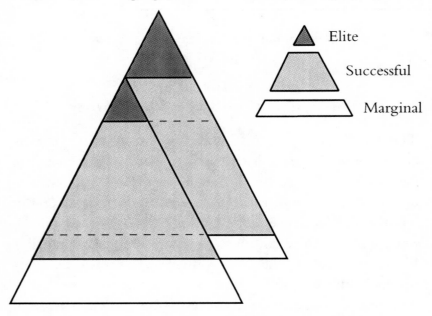

Social Strata in an Ever-Advancing Civilization

this static analysis of power and privilege obsolete. Yes, there is a pyramid of power and it is likely there always will be. But what has been left out of the analysis is that this pyramid is constantly changing, rising to new levels of human success, comfort, and advantage undreamed of in earlier ages. It is readily discernible that the common man in the industrial world now lives more comfortably than the kings of even the recent past.

In spite of the fact that we can recognize this reality, we are still locked into the outdated notions of competition for power hierarchies that no longer have meaning. It is ironic that as the pyramid of power moves up, those who hold on to their old notions of power and privilege will actually be left behind.

Power in an Ever-Advancing Civilization

The only constructive response is for everyone to join together in reaching for new heights. Even those people once considered of the "lowest strata," competing for power, are confused by this new reality. Instead of reaching for new heights, they, too, often struggle to displace the old power, even as those in the old power structure struggle to maintain their obsolete power. When those at the lower levels finally (if unequally) become successful in the "old sense" they feel cheated because it is then obvious that their achievements are hollow—that the real apex of power still eludes them.

This new reality of privilege and power means that poverty is no longer necessary, that we can first imagine and then achieve the prosperity of all humankind. If we address the true issues of social and economic advancement, we will start recognizing an ever-expanding base of resources and capacities. We will then be able to take into account the constant upward movement of the pyramid of power and learn to take full advantage of that movement for the benefit of all. We will all then move with surprising alacrity to new levels of power for all.

This is the power of peace in action, to bring prosperity. It's a process of iteration. The first wave came during the Industrial Revolution, with the establishment of the middle class. As technology advanced, an increasing number of lower-level tasks required no human support, and we all moved on to higher levels of employment. With the dawn of the information age, we see an entirely new meaning to the idea that knowledge is power. As increasing percentages of the society have access to ever-widening sources of knowledge, we are all moving up again to new levels of prosperity. Once we learn to control armed conflict and find peaceful ways to resolve disputes, still more resources will become available to promote the prosperity of all humankind.

Leadership

New models of leadership are emerging everywhere—in the workplace and the governing council chambers of America. One of the common features of these new models is shared decision making. Leaders are urged to give everyone a genuine voice while retaining ultimate responsibility for leadership. This power is defined and shared both formally and informally.

But current leaders have difficulty accepting these new concepts. They see their power as being threatened. They fear loss of power and control as others are empowered to lead and decide.

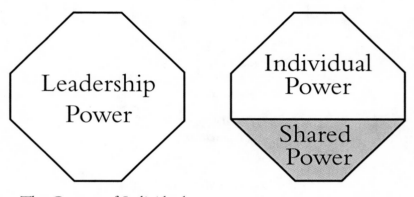

The Concept of Individual Power

Sharing Static Power

The Real Power of Shared Leadership

Too often, leaders fail to understand the new reality that shared leadership produces. As more members of an organization are brought into the power structure, the total power of the organization is increased. Any leader is constrained by the effective span of control he or she can exert. With shared leadership, shared vision, and shared responsibility, the effective span of control is vastly increased. The sharing of power has produced more power! More power for "the people," but more power for the leader as well.

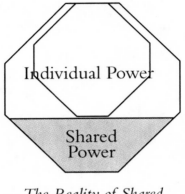

The Reality of Shared Leadership

Education and the Power of Peace

It is the power held in education that has the ability to change our awareness of the new realities that are already upon us. For the first time in human history, the comfort of one human being does not depend on the discomfort of another. Servants are almost unknown in modern Western societies. Marginal lives are no longer necessary. Support roles are achieving new status. Executives are finding less need for secretaries. The roles of administrative assistants are constantly being redefined to take on more scope. Differentiation of tasks and responsibilities is the inevitable result. In the health professions, in business, and finally in education new roles will emerge. New sources of power will be identified and shared. And the new reality of the potential of win-win strategies will finally make peace possible. We will gradually come to realize that we all have more to win when we all work together. Then we will create more power for the peace and prosperity for the totality of humankind.

PART 2
Solutions That Are Possible in the Real World

Year-Round School

Is it in our interest to have year-round schools? There are regional interests, of course. For instance, schools near resort areas supply low-cost seasonal personnel. It will take creativity to meet the needs of regions and still have the necessary coordination for effective year-round schooling. We must be able to count on what kids learn each year and develop a curriculum with longer school days or years in mind. The schedule to accomplish this will be a matter of local variation, but with support a longer school day or year merits it.

Whether all school staff should be on twelve-month contracts should be debated also. Many teachers now choose the profession because of summer flexibility, but that may be too high a price to pay if it blocks effective scheduling and staffing.

One possible pattern for year-round schooling could work in such a way that everyone would have seven weeks off at varying times during the school year. One way for this to work is to have four thirteen-week cycles in a year with a one-week vacation every twelve weeks. In each of those quarterly cycles we could have nine weeks of school with three weeks of remediation, enrichment, or vacation. Everyone would attend the nine-week program, teachers and students would be there for three of the four three-week remediation and enrichment programs, and everybody would have one of the three-week sessions off. So everybody would have four individual weeks of planned vacation plus an additional three weeks from one remediation and enrichment session.

These are just a few of the possibilities waiting to be examined. But in order to find out how and whether year-round schools work, we need to support them.

We must realize that schools are not now effectively organized. We need to try different experimental organization patterns. For example, there is research evidence that suggests that if a high school has about 1,800 kids, it is better to divide those kids into four "houses" so that they would have a smaller, more personal and closely knit reference group. Another alternative is to develop groups of about one hundred kids that share classes and teachers. This way the teachers and kids get to know each other well. This is a popular pattern at middle school level, but, for some reason, is rarely used in high schools. There is evidence that one of the barriers to learning is the feeling of anonymity present in many large schools. Elementary schools have successfully experimented with "looping," where teachers stay with the same class for two or three years. Evidence is needed to overcome the weight of tradition.

How Long Should the School Day Be?

The length of the school day as well as the length and timing of the school year requires new perspectives. Some schools might open at seven in the morning and not close until ten at night. Kids and teachers could come and go, with some teachers coming in at eight and leaving at five, and other teachers coming in at one and leaving at ten. There is nothing sacred—or particularly effective—about having everybody at school on the same schedule. The school would probably serve the society better if students, staff, parents, and community members have flexible schedules. There's a great deal of talk concerning the importance of community involvement in schools. We must experiment with organizational patterns to encourage this participation.

If a school were open from 7:00 A.M. until 10:00 P.M., it would be able to serve the community in new ways. Parents with inflexible schedules would find it easier to keep in touch with teachers. Students would have somewhere to be when their parents are not home rather than on the streets or unsupervised at home. Also, since each individual has a personal peak time for learning, we would be better able to utilize this capability. There is brain research, for example, that suggests that teenagers have natural sleep cycles, which fit later bedtimes and later wake-up times. The schools could also be open to the community for all kinds of adult education. We aren't sure what patterns will be effective, but it is worth systematic investigation of many alternatives.

Class Size and Group Work

We need to try different experimental instructional patterns. For example, we would like to find out if there is some benefit in having large-group instruction in high school. If you have five hundred kids in U.S. history, it might be useful once in a while to do something with all five hundred of those kids in an auditorium. This could be useful in terms of saving instructional resources. Every time you have one class with all five hundred, you save as much as fifteen hours of teaching time. It would take that much more time to teach those kids thirty at a time in classrooms. You now have fifteen additional hours of teacher time available to do something else. A combination of large and small groups would be optimal. Sometimes teachers could be dealing with groups of ten or twelve instead of always dealing with groups of twenty-five. If teachers are going to try such experimentation, a developmental staff and resources are needed to support them. Of course, they can't expect to get it right the first time or to have the same instructional pattern work under all conditions.

Redefining the Basics: SCANS

In the 1980s, Japan's economy seemed invulnerable, and the United States. became convinced it couldn't compete in a rapidly changing world. There was a great deal of talk of being "world class" in everything we did—including education. Employers became vocal about the lack of skills "average" workers exhibited. High school graduates

73

seemed to lack the skills to compete. Corporations released statistics showing that applicants couldn't meet entry-level standards. A cry went up: education was failing the nation.

The Department of Labor's response was to appoint the Secretary's Commission for the Achievement of Necessary Skills (SCANS). This group focused on what skills the worker of the twenty-first century would need.

The SCANS report, released in 1989, is extraordinary because it defines the skills that are appropriate for college-bound students as well as for vocational students. It offers an important template for redefining basic education, but its influence was limited first for political reasons (a change in political party control) and because we found that America wasn't as far behind other nations as we feared. Our education remains obsolete, but other nations' education is obsolete as well. Here is what SCANS recommends for workers in the twenty-first century; we think it is an excellent starting point for the redefinition of the basics.

A Three-Part Foundation for Skills
Basic Skills

Reads, writes, performs arithmetic and mathematical operations, listens, and speaks.

- Reading—locates, understands, and interprets written information in prose and in documents such as manuals, graphs, and schedules.
- Writing—communicates thoughts, ideas, information, and messages in writing; and creates documents

74

such as letters, directions, manuals, reports, graphs, and flow charts.

• Arithmetic/Mathematics—performs basic computations and approaches practical problems by choosing appropriately from a variety of mathematical techniques.

• Listening—receives, attends to, interprets, and responds to verbal messages and other cues

• Speaking—organizes ideas and communicates orally.

Thinking Skills
(Glass half full or half empty)

Thinks creatively, makes decisions, solves problems, visualizes, knows how to learn, and reasons.

• Creative Thinking—generates new ideas.

• Decision Making—specifies goals and constraints, generates alternatives, considers risks, and evaluates and chooses best alternative.

• Problem Solving—recognizes problems and devises and implements plan of action.

• Seeing Things in the Mind's Eye—organizes and processes symbols, pictures, graphs, objects, and other information.

• Knowing How to Learn—uses efficient learning techniques to acquire and apply new knowledge and skills.

• Reasoning—discovers a rule or principle underlying the relationship between two or more objects and applies it when solving a problem.

Personal Qualities

Displays responsibility, self-esteem, sociability, self-management, and integrity and honesty.

- Responsibility—exerts a high level of effort and perseveres toward goal attainment.
- Self-esteem—believes in own self-worth and maintains a positive view of self.
- Sociability—demonstrates understanding, friendliness, adaptability, empathy, and politeness in group settings.
- Self-Management—assesses self accurately, sets personal goals, monitors progress, and exhibits self-control.
- Integrity/Honesty—chooses ethical courses of action.

Our Lack of Response to SCANS

Few disagree with SCANS. There were no strong voices raised against it. But no one paid very much attention to it, either. This is the paradox of educational reform—serious, credible reforms remain untried. In the current system they cannot be tested because they call for too many changes simultaneously.

To take SCANS seriously and see if schooling could be reoriented to achieve SCANS competencies in a predictable way would require a major effort. To implement SCANS on a trial basis would require the designation of experimental schools, the redefinition of curriculum, the retraining of teachers, and substantial resources. Unfortunately, there aren't any forums for debating the merits of SCANS and no way to implement any reform efforts we decide to try. Our proposed National Experimental Schools Administration would provide a way to begin.

If such an experiment were undertaken it would require at least a decade to implement thoroughly enough to make a judgment of its worth. This is one reason that establishing a national experimental school system is required for real educational reform. Without some large-scale experimentation we are condemned to superficial reform without much real success. By continuing the present educational framework we are forced to consider only the reform measures that fit within its known-to-be-obsolete boundaries.

SCANS in the Curriculum

The SCANS report is not the complete curriculum. In fact it is silent on how to teach many of its skills, and, most important, it doesn't take into account how its skills relate to general education. Even though this is the case, SCANS does not compete with traditional subjects but rather it complements them.

How would the SCANS curriculum fit with current curriculum requirements? The current curriculum, though unstated, is very rigid and very packed. Everyone knows what it is. English (including reading and language arts), social studies, math, and science are the big four, and everything else is considered elective—even frills. There are lots of national standards, all of which are "unofficial." We cite the math standards developed by the National Council of the Teachers of Mathematics when we need them, but no one really feels bound by them. Other curriculum associations have proposed national standards as well, and the good news is that we at least are gaining a consciousness for the need for common standards, even though we don't trust anyone to develop them and don't want to be bound by them. We believe there's room for greater efficiency within the curriculum. That, however, is unlikely to be enough. What could or should be left out to make room for the new elements? Should the school day or school year or both be lengthened to accommodate the new curriculum? Tough choices would have to be made.

In the past, it has been almost impossible to remove any of the current curricula, even when we have a need to add important new elements. Geography, for example, has been a "national goal" for a decade with little result. The curriculum is stuffed, yet still we add more. In fact, even without SCANS, we need to add more. There needs to be more emphasis on the arts, the history/culture of the Pacific Rim nations, nutrition, and the environment, as just a few examples. Having a new curriculum, which must be different from the current one, is bound to make us uncomfortable. We must try different alternatives, and we believe that a thorough trial of SCANS should be a part of that effort.

Teachers

The key to effective education is having effective teachers. We haven't done a very good job of creating a profession staffed by effective teachers.

We stand at a moment of poignant opportunity—and

likely missed opportunity. For two decades the teaching profession has been "filled." Teachers hired during the baby boom of the sixties have been going through the ranks, and relatively few positions have been available. Now this large cohort of sixties' teachers is retiring, and we are facing a teacher shortage nationally, just at the time when there is the political will to hire at least some new teachers to reduce class size. Consider the irony. As a nation we have been complaining about the relative low quality of teachers. (We believe unreasonably so.) This was in part because during the teacher shortage of the sixties we had to hire almost anyone who was breathing. Not many really bad teachers were hired or retained, but lots of teachers with relatively low aspiration levels have populated the profession for the past quarter century.

Now, once again, we have to hire large numbers of teachers—committing ourselves to the next quarter century of the profession. Once again we will hire almost anyone who comes through the door. Why can't we now redefine the profession, accepting that it will take time for the new standards to percolate down through the system, but making the dramatic investment that will build the kind of educational program we yearn for in the future? This is why we need a massive infusion of funds:

- to redefine the kind of person who is attracted to teaching,
- to redefine teacher education—starting with extensive clinical practice under close supervision for one or two years,
- to redefine the scope and delivery of in-service teacher

education to keep our teachers up to date and provide them with support, and
- to redefine the way teachers interact with each other to generate entirely new levels of feedback and encouragement through regular visitation and mutual observation.

Elements of Teacher Empowerment

Shared Decision Making

Teachers are "knowledge workers." This concept describes the modern workplace, where often the teachers—"workers"—have expertise that the principal—"boss"—does not have. The management issue is to find ways to lead knowledge workers and to capitalize on their expertise while retaining the authentic leadership roles of management. Teachers often know more than their principals about detailed aspects of school management from day to day, and it is one of the challenges of school reform to find ways to involve teachers in the leadership of the school. One of the most pervasive practices in schools has been site-based management.

There are mixed findings about the effectiveness of site-based management. The premise is excellent: Empower teachers by involving them in the governance of the school. The results are mixed because of a host of variables that make it difficult to decide whether the idea, or its implementation, is flawed. First, it hasn't been clear what the authority of a management council includes. In theory, the creation of school councils has been associated with decentralization. The flaw in this thinking is that it involves two separate issues—decentralization and teacher empowerment. Teachers can be more involved in school governance even under traditional centralized control. Also, large bureaucracies make it difficult for individual schools to function optimally.

Another flaw in site-based management is that teachers have been given management responsibility but no additional resources or reduction in other responsibilities. Teacher participation in governance has often translated into more work for them.

A third problem is that it is unclear what authority a school council has. Principals usually have veto power, and teachers sometimes end up feeling that they have invested time for nothing. Principals are responsible for the overall well-being of the schools they serve, and thus they must have authority to shape the institution. But there are realms of authority that they can and should authentically delegate to teachers and management councils. The issue is not the technical point of authority but the functioning relationship the principal has with his or her staff. Shared decision making is the vision of future leadership. It is understood that the employee on the line has insights that are important, so when management finds ways to use this insight, everyone wins. Sharing power doesn't necessarily reduce the power of the principal, it increases the power of the organization to govern itself and respond to crisis and opportunity.

Respect

Respect is an intangible. It must be earned, but it can also be fostered. Teachers need to develop self-confidence if they are to function effectively. At present the society gives teachers many cues that they are not respected. The cry for external examinations is one example. When we have the right kind of teachers, we won't need such exams on an individual level, only sampling to see how large populations compare to test the basic skills of students. If we respected teachers' judgment, external examinations would not be necessary. Low pay is another such sign. The fact that all teachers are "below" all school administrators, even budget managers, is yet another example. The lack of trust that parents show teachers when they defend their children's misbehavior and challenge the teachers' authority further erodes teacher respect. Part of the problem is simply that we live in a society where trust in our institutions in general has weakened. But we all pay a high price for the lack of respect for teachers

Instructional Resources

Instructional resources can be as simple as adequate paper and chalk, or as complex as access to networks and databases with computer support. Currently, many teachers spend personal funds for instructional materials because their schools lack, or they have only limited access to, the equipment they need. Think what a huge difference it makes to have an overhead projector in your classroom rather than one that must be requisitioned from the media center.

Teacher Compensation

What are teachers worth? Not all teachers perform at the same level. And it is difficult to determine which teacher is more valuable. The teacher who can turn one child around from a dropout to a success is a priceless asset to society. But today, the teacher who can write grants may generate enough resources to support his or her salary several times over. How about the teacher who can motivate gifted students to excel, or the teacher who is adept at working with children with special needs, or the teacher who makes sure average students acquire skills that will make them productive, or the teacher who teaches remedial students successfully?

Who is more valuable, the teacher who teaches English and communications skills, the teacher who teaches nutrition, or the teacher who prepares her students to protect the natural world around them? Is the teacher who teaches good manners in kindergarten less valuable than the counselor who helps a student select a college? Is the head football coach more valuable when he wins than when he loses?

We must develop master teachers in all aspects of teaching and learning. They, in turn, will redefine schools and schooling. They will partner with those who bring other skills to the school, from software developers to administrators, from business managers to researchers, from curriculum designers to community developers, but teachers are the school's heart. The teaching profession must be restructured so that the best teachers have the greatest responsibility and compensation.

As we stated before, we believe that for the teaching profession to take its rightful place in society, three things must occur:

1. The highest-paid teacher is paid as much as the highest-paid administrator.
2. The highest-paid preschool teacher is paid the same as the highest-paid college professor.
3. The most effective teachers are paid on the same level as the most effective doctors, lawyers, and engineers.

Lifelong In-Service Teacher Education

At present, on-the-job teacher education is simply a series of sometimes useful, sometimes boring lectures. Systematic upgrading of skills has never been built in to the profession. We know how much knowledge is changing, so there is wide agreement that teachers need systematic retraining. The current system does not allow this. Teachers take classes and complete degree programs on their own time. In return, they are supposedly rewarded—with higher pay schedules. This is true to an extent, but there are better ways to ensure an up-to-date teaching force. Rather than leaving teachers on their own to determine what knowledge they need, the system ought to offer training as a feature of the teacher's schedules. There are many ways to accomplish this. Teachers can be released during school on a regular basis. There could be multiple, simultaneous courses, each meeting one or two hours per week or month. Teachers could be released for a two- or three-week period of intensive study. Clearly, in order to develop significant in-service opportunities, schedules must be flexible. The current practice, which gives one teacher sole responsibility for classes five days a week for a semester or year, does not fit in-service needs. Teachers cannot be senior professionals without extensive opportunity for upgrading their knowledge.

In addition to considering long-term in-service training options, we propose immediate funding of a massive in-service teacher training initiative on the Internet.

In-service training materials available on the Internet are multiplying rapidly. For example, WETA public television in New York has excellent in-service programs in math and science where teachers can find sample lesson plans, ideas for classroom activities, and suggested test items. But these programs lack coordination, they are not used systematically by most school districts, and the weak and untrained teachers, the teachers most in need, are unlikely even to know about them.

We want to offer teachers $20 per hour for up to two hours a week, to systematically upgrade both their content and methodological skills on the Internet. This would provide teachers about $2,000 per year as a training incentive. We think most teachers would take advantage of such an opportunity.

More Powerful Teacher Education

As we said before, current standards of teacher education are antiquated, formed by nineteenth-century notions about women and work. Although the nature of the profession has changed, little about the training has. Teacher education is still basically a one-year add-on to undergraduate liberal arts degrees. This is not enough, and we must do better.

Much rhetoric has shown the value of clinical experiences as a part of teacher education: the opportunity for teachers in training to get actual classroom experience, watching, helping, teaching under supervision, and finally teaching on their own with access to help. The fact is that education professors are not motivated to spend time supervising classroom teachers.

Micro-teaching, which is a short, five-minute single-concept lesson with three or four teacher colleagues acting the role of students has been demonstrated to be effective for generations, but in recent years micro-teaching has declined because earlier models required complex schedules and intensive supervising. New concepts of micro-teaching, which empower teachers to supervise each other in simulated lessons, are easily managed. There is no doubt that micro-teaching is a good entry-level clinical experience.

We need to establish closer ties between university teacher-training programs and the public schools. Such relationships are complex, even controversial, but teacher training calls for access to practical experiences. This should begin with observation, move to supplemental teaching tasks, on to work with individual students, then to limited instructional responsibility in other teachers' classes, then to closely supervised full teaching responsibility. This supervision should continue during the first years of a teacher's practice.

University professors must be more closely identified with schools. Too often professors have little contact with real classrooms. Master teachers must be trained to become trusted senior partners in the teaching process. The concept of a laboratory school associated with a teacher-training program is outdated. A much broader school-university relationship is required. The concept of professional development schools where long-term, close ties are established between individual schools and a nearby university is a promising new pattern of training, but it is still evolving, and there are obstacles including turf battles, finance, and integration of school with university-based training.

The real starting point for twenty-first-century training is to equate the resources for teaching with those of other senior professions. A three-year training program, in which the first year is combined with undergraduate study and the second and third years incorporate increasing responsibilities is a reasonable starting point. In academic terms, either a master's degree or a Certificate of Advanced Study, one year beyond the master's degree, is an appropriate entry level for professional teachers. With new patterns of staffing, associate teachers with less training could work under the supervision of professional teachers in collaborative roles, but not with complete responsibility for their classes.

Consequences for Good and Bad Performance

At present, there are no consequences for good and bad performance. Short of being fired, all teachers are locked into a system of automatic yearly salary raises. This has long been recognized as unsatisfactory, but the single-salary schedule where all teachers are paid the same based on their training and experience, is so pervasive in American education that alternatives are hard to consider.

As with many changes, teacher compensation is tied to other teaching practices. Differentiated staffing is one of the most promising alternatives. For several decades the ideas of differentiated staffing and career ladders, different levels of responsibility with different levels of pay, and merit pay, which is paying outstanding teachers more without changing their responsibilities, have struggled to become viable. It's important to pay outstanding teachers more, but formally identifying the outstanding teachers without changing their responsibilities creates more problems than it solves, because parents, understandably, will put even more pressure on the school to put their kids in the classes with outstanding "merit" teachers.

We believe that differentiated staffing, a new concept of teacher roles with many levels of compensation and responsibility, is needed, with teachers promoted to senior roles based on performance, not seniority. We are not likely to develop the best pattern of staffing immediately, and that is why we feel strongly about trying experimental incentives such as the following.

Promotion Within the Classroom

Part of the change required for proper compensation is to accept the necessity of promotion for teachers within a classroom and changing the responsibilities of classroom teachers. The largest barrier to such promotions is the current universal practice that all teachers have responsibility over a class for an entire semester. If classes become a team responsibility, it becomes possible for master teachers to remain involved as classroom teachers, but not necessarily on a day-to-day basis, while undertaking other senior professional activities. Now it is all or nothing. Either you are a teacher or you are an administrator. This must be changed. The teacher internship program implemented in Brunswick County, Virginia, as a part of the ACTT Now (Aligning Certificate Training with Technology) project funded by the U.S. Department of Education, is one possible answer. A semester or yearlong internship in lieu of student teaching makes it possible to release master teachers part-time to visit other classrooms and undertake other professional responsibilities. In the case of Brunswick County, master teachers will be developing new modular curriculum materials using lots of technology.

Time for Reflection

One characteristic of a senior profession is opportunity for reflection, because reflection allows for professional improvement and is not facilitated by frenzied responsibility. Many teachers report a frenzied professional experience characterized by competing responsibilities and a lack of time. It isn't too strong to say that most teachers don't teach up to their ability. They don't have the time to do all requirements, from paperwork to lesson planning, from paper correction to planning remedial strategies, from updating skills to calling parents, and from planning lectures to designing inventive evaluation strategies.

We cannot provide time for reflection without rethinking how teachers spend their day. Experimentation will be required to achieve this, but the first step is to acknowledge its importance.

Support for Risk Taking

We live in a time of change, but change requires risk. Schools have never been known for taking risks, and in fact minimizing risk has been of the highest values. Risk is not only necessary, but inevitable. We must learn to encourage risk taking and let teachers know that risks are supported. We must help teachers understand how to learn from their mistakes.

Professional Discretion

Personal discretion is one of the hallmarks of a senior profession. When we examine current teaching practices, we expose how limited the teacher's role actually is. Professional discretion has many dimensions. Many senior professionals can, within limits, set their own schedules. Teachers should be able to miss classes, arrive late, or leave early for professional reasons, but to have that discretion, there must be new support systems in place. Again, instruction should not be tied to the presence of a single teacher, and with a teaching staff, it need not be. In addition, teachers should be able to spend time with individual students and to select materials. Furthermore, teachers need access to petty cash to purchase supplemental supplies and small equipment. Teachers should not worry about having paper, or access to a phone or copy machine. If we want teachers to be senior professionals, we have to provide them with the tools and resources accorded other professionals.

Increased Collegiality

Now teacher isolation is the norm. Rarely do teachers observe other classes to offer or receive suggestions from colleagues. This situation must be changed. The new 2+2 performance appraisal system, also implemented in Brunswick County, will allow all teachers to observe each other at least once a week. "2+2" stands for two compliments and two suggestions. A teacher observes another class long enough to make two solid compliments and two suggestions for improvement. The theory is that no class is without merit, and every class can benefit from suggestions.

Suggestions for improvement may or may not be criticisms; they may be proposals for alternatives, timing, or examples. It has taken time for teachers to get used to observing and being observed. There is a strong teaching culture that discourages any kind of criticism. Nonetheless

the results have been encouraging, and now most participants in the program seek out feedback from their peers—
even in other schools and at other grade levels.

Role in Decision Making

At present teachers are at the bottom of the food chain.
They are so accustomed to doing as they are told, they don't
notice how small a voice they have in decision making.
Teachers often have good suggestions for guidance coun-
selors for the help and support of students who are having
difficulty. And teachers see ways to improve school management—everything from bus schedules to attendance procedures. Usually these ideas are the fodder for faculty lounge
gossip and rarely are considered in any serious way. When
we give teachers opportunities for educational leadership,
they often aren't very comfortable, and the effort usually
ends before real power has been consolidated. Until the role
of the teacher is redefined to allow for time away from students, there is little chance for alternatives that involve
teachers in decision making because any involvement in
leadership is added on to an already unreasonably packed
workday.

It is unreasonable to expect that the teacher's role in decision making will be instantly transformed. No one really
knows what the limits should be, but if teachers are key to
the success of schools, their opinions must be effectively
heard and acted on.

Offering Self-Designed Elective Classes

One important "badge" of teacher empowerment is the right to develop and offer unique courses. Teachers should be able to develop and offer elective courses. Offering courses dear to the hearts of teachers will enrich the school. Again, the solution must be systemic. If we accept national standards that we are confident can be met, we will have the confidence to offer teacher-defined electives. The joy inherent in sharing a favorite intellectual passion will likely stimulate higher performance by teacher and student alike. Why is this such an unusual suggestion? Using the resources unique to the school will enhance performance. Such individualized courses should be elective but scheduled in creative ways that allow them to fit into crowded teacher and student schedules on an individual or small-group basis. There are many ways to develop such unique offerings, but we need to have the opportunity to experiment with their development.

Strengthening Mentorship

Senior professionals should mentor their junior colleagues. There is great satisfaction that comes from sharing experience, and value in having an anchor to turn to in times of stress. Some mentoring goes on now, but it is haphazard at best. It should become institutionalized through the formal assignment of new teachers to mentors and, as differentiated staffing takes hold, the assignment of master teachers to supervise less competent and more junior levels of the teaching staff.

Incentives for Entering the Teaching Profession

We talk about attracting the best students to teaching and we have established minimum standards, but incentives remain mediocre and illusory. Stable employment is one of the greatest incentives. Freedom during the summertime is another. The lure of early release of students and a short workday is still another. The environment of the classroom is another incentive, but only for the right classrooms in the right schools. Compensation is definitely not an incentive, nor is professional empowerment.

Many new teachers leave the profession after they find their illusions are not supported. Freedom during the summertime means finding another job to increase compensation. The short workday is an illusion. Research has shown the average week for teachers to be about 54 hours. After class there are papers to correct, lessons to plan, parents to call, kids to counsel, and materials to round up. The selection of classes to teach offers the wrong incentives. Teachers flock to the upper-level honors classes to teach motivated students. Classes with remedial students are unpopular with most teachers, because resources and support are lacking and numbers are large.

Teachers must be paid more. They need staff support. They need freedom to come and go without jeopardizing student achievement. Their voices need to be heard. They need to develop feelings of collegiality. In other words, they need to gain a sense of personal empowerment. Only then will we be able to recruit the top graduates into the profession of teaching.

Achieving Empowerment

Should the teaching profession have a share of the most talented members of society? Obviously, the answer is yes. But until now, the barriers to achieving that obvious objective have been insurmountable. We challenge our readers to envision a society where teachers perform at the highest level of competence for their students' welfare. Teachers should help design and implement the training programs for those entering the profession. Teachers should have a large voice in what is taught and how. Teacher empowerment should be one of the principal experimental arenas for the experimental schools in NESA.

More Expertise

We are still uncertain what teachers need to know to be effective teachers. Chris, now a math teacher in an urban school, serves as a good example of this. The Virginia State legislature passed a law requiring Chris to have more mathematics. He had enough mathematics to successfully receive his bachelor's degree in aeronautical engineering from Penn State, but had to take an extra year in his graduate preparation as a teacher because he didn't have enough of the "right kind of math," whatever that is! It remains unclear to us how this extra year of math preparation has helped Chris deal with thirty-five kids who don't want to learn algebra.

It's popular to require teachers to be experts in the subjects they teach—and while teachers should know their subject areas well, it is equally important that they are taught how to learn and given the opportunity to add to their knowledge as they teach. If we want teachers to remain up to date in their subject fields, teachers must be given the resources and time to develop a habit of perpetual learning.

Much of the criticism of the lack of teacher preparation, particularly in math, is uninformed. Many current teachers of math are not prepared as math teachers. Established standards for the content preparation of math teachers have long been reasonable. But because so many teachers are not properly prepared (a result of the unattractive nature of the teaching profession discussed at length elsewhere in this book) it has given the illusion that more math should be required. This has led to ridiculous and ill-advised requirements for the preparation of math teachers—a politically popular way to "solve" the problems of poor student performance. Colleges of education bear the brunt of the blame, though they are not even responsible for the academic preparation of the teachers they train. The rhetoric is that too much time is given to pedagogical training. The reality is that not enough time is given to pedagogical training, but much of the training now offered in colleges of education is inadequate and out of date.

A recent study of teacher roles by Dr. James Onderdonk demonstrated that parents, the public, and teachers themselves consider it more important for teachers to be facilitators of learning than content experts, yet the legislatures and politicians have found it expedient to blame teachers' lack of subject-matter expertise for weak student performance. This comes down to the argument concerning which is more important—subject area or methodology.

It is not surprising that the movement to require teachers to be subject-matter experts has not produced any results. Why require elementary teachers to major in a single subject when they will teach six or eight? To get around state regulations requiring teachers to have an "academic major," colleges have become creative. They have begun programming elementary teachers into interdisciplinary majors, which were designed for very different purposes. This gets around the law but it is a misuse of the available resources. And it doesn't really give teachers substantially more knowledge in academic areas than an undergraduate major in education. We need more time to train senior elementary teachers. We need to develop staffing patterns that allow subject-area specialization in the elementary schools. But most of all, we need to give more attention to sound methodological training that colleges of education should offer. We also need to redefine the courses prospective teachers take in their teaching subjects. University mathematics professors are not likely to be interested in teaching what the mathematics teachers will need for elementary and secondary schools. Most university mathematics professors are not even aware of what math is being taught in schools, let alone the problems teachers face while teaching it. Most often, university professors themselves lack any methodological preparation. Isn't it strange that effective teaching is not required at the university level? Many of the most exalted professors are not particularly good teachers, even though we know that the same principles of learning apply to college students as well as to kindergartners.

Professors of mathematics—indeed of any discipline—have little career incentive to collaborate in teacher preparation because their promotion and tenure depend on their scholarly production in their own subject areas and seldom on their service to teachers. And it is the rare college professor of math who is interested in doing research on the teaching of mathematics in classrooms. Our colleges and universities need more joint appointments between academic and education departments, though at present such arrangements usually place the individual professor in jeopardy in both departments because his research interests lie outside conventional academic boundaries. Teachers need academic preparation in their teaching subjects that is closely related to what they actually teach. Teachers should know the academic disciplines they teach well beyond the levels at which they will teach them in the classroom. They need to achieve a balance: establishing a base of solid academic preparation without placing undue emphasis on theoretical, abstract concepts relevant only to those planning to do advanced research.

Of what, specifically, should a teacher's academic preparation consist? We believe that issue cannot be fully addressed until schools increase the total training time for teachers. Not only do colleges of education need to overhaul teacher education curricula; fundamental reform is needed in all academic departments. Such sweeping reform is unlikely so long as professors are awarded promotions and tenure solely on the basis of theoretical research conducted in narrow disciplines. Is it sensible for English professors who have never seen the inside of a high-school or elementary-school English/Language Arts classroom to make decisions about the subject preparation required of English teachers? What ends up happening is that English teachers simply have the same or nearly the same academic preparation as any English major. There are promising developments of university teacher education councils that provide opportunity for faculty in the academic disciplines and the college of education to interact. But academic professors still rarely get into school classrooms.

Colleges of education are equally obsolete in their approach. There are no villains, and everyone is trying to improve, but we continue to be frustrated by the circumstances that constrain real reform. The real problem is that we are still trying to train teachers in one year. We also have to face the reality that universities have been using colleges of education to subsidize more elite professional training in engineering and the sciences. Large numbers of teacher candidates swell the ranks of university enrollments and compensate for the lower numbers in other professional training programs. Rarely do colleges of education receive the same funding ratios as other professional schools. This must change if we want to reinvent the profession of teaching.

Staffing Patterns

We also want to implement experimental staffing patterns such as differentiated staffing, mentoring, part-time personnel, and volunteers. We would like to explore the concept of the teacher and teaching staff. We need to experiment with different kinds of teaching teams and working styles. We could experiment with teaching teams across grade levels, disciplines, across schools, and with full- and part-time community involvement. Our vision of the future features the teacher as a senior professional helped by many folks and in charge of directing resources to maximize learning. The current situation, in which teachers are the lowest-level professionals in the school, doesn't appeal to us.

The typical school hates part-time people because of the administrative mess they cause. However, when used effectively, they can be extraordinarily valuable. For example, what a wonderful resource it would be for a local sculptor to come in and teach sculpting one or two classes a day. As it is now, sculptors have to teach full-time or not at all, with the exception of some adult education classes. Is this to the advantage of kids and their learning? First, it would be good financial support for the sculptors, who find it tough to make a living in our society. Second, it would benefit the kids while allowing the sculptor time to do his or her own work.

In addition to the part-time master sculptor, we need master teachers full-time in the school. Would we be willing to pay for such master teachers after they are trained? Are we willing to construct careers for teachers to attract the best and the brightest? Will we have the courage to try out multiple approaches to differentiated staffing, thus learning what kind of instructional design and support staff will make master teachers most effective? We can't expect all teachers to be master teachers, but those who are are a resource to be protected, nurtured, and well compensated for their efforts. There are many studies that show that a lower adult-child ratio is more important than having a small class size with a single teacher. We haven't had enough experience with models to know what the ideal mix of professional teachers and support staff is, what size of classes is best, and whether the ideal varies according to grade level, subject area, or individual teaching style. It will be very expensive to learn these things, but the potential rewards are enormous. Billions of dollars are required if we are to explore the vast new frontiers of knowledge that lie inside the classroom door.

For example, we agree teachers must be comfortable with new technologies, but there are professors of education (happily a rapidly shrinking number) who are still not computer literate and who refuse to learn as a matter of academic freedom. Dwight Allen requires students to hand in various assignments through e-mail accounts, to take their quizzes "on line," and to use the Internet for their term projects. But other professors teaching the same introductory subject have no such requirements. These unequal situations are created well before college. Some students are computer literate before they reach high school; some have no exposure to technology before college—a part of the larger digital divide we are addressing head-on elsewhere in this book. When a class on introduction to computers is taught, some students are bored with it because they have already learned it as a by-product of other study, while other students struggle to keep up. This is not the end of the problem, however. There are many university student-teaching supervisors who are not computer literate. So even when student teachers are in classrooms with appropriate technology, some supervisors are helpless to critique their performance in that area. Getting everyone on the same "technological" wavelength is almost impossible. In order to do this we must have a path to a predictable level of technology in schools. Teachers must be taught by a technologically literate faculty who, in turn, are trained to keep up with new technologies. Even if we commit ourselves to decades of solid experimentation, it will cost billions of dollars if we have any chance of doing it right.

The vision of an effective teaching profession seems almost impossible to achieve when we consider the reality we face. The preparation program at Old Dominion University is lauded for its efforts to provide early experience for its teachers in training. It is typical, however, for students to call the schools only to have a staff member say that they are having difficulty finding a teacher who will accept an "observer." It is nonsense to develop a profession where teachers are reluctant to make teaching a public act. It's also unfortunate that teachers are not trained to use all resources, even one-time observers to enrich instruction. When teachers develop a concept of the teacher and his or her staff, the mentality will change as teachers become more alert to the value of temporary and part-time resources.

Again, there are no villains. The teachers who don't want interruption are often competent and conscientious; they simply have been trained to have a different set of expectations. Their concept of professional service has become obsolete. They have no concept of the teacher and his or her staff. They are isolated, and they have come to like it that way.

Because teachers rarely receive visitors, they rarely receive any feedback about their performance. We can do better, and there are models extant that can be developed to overcome teacher isolation. One of these is the 2+2 program that we cited earlier. First developed in Namibia and used in China before it was brought to the United States, the 2 + 2 classrooms has received strong, positive endorsement from the teachers in the PRIME project in Norfolk. After an initial reluctance to both give and receive compliments and suggestions, teachers report they have come to treasure the critique performance. They get new ideas both from visiting and being visited. The only drawback is finding the means to release teachers from their classes to visit other teachers. If there were a "staff" in every class, the temporary absence of the teacher occasionally would be little trouble.

New Teachers—Worst Kids

Although it is important to discuss what is needed to create the premium learning environment, it is equally important to discuss the realities faced by today's teachers. Take, for example, Chris, who was a graduate assistant before he went to an inner-city high school as an intern teacher. Chris won university awards as the outstanding graduate assistant of the year. Chris is an idealist. He wants all his students to succeed and he is ready to do whatever it takes to help this happen.

As a new teacher he has five classes. Two of them are "upper-end" classes—geometry for ninth graders. In these classes the students are motivated and want to go to college. He enjoys teaching them and they are doing very well. The other three are "lower-end" classes and are his largest. With about thirty-five students in each of these classes, Chris estimates that there are ten who want to learn and another five who will occasionally try. In addition, each class may contain as many as ten special education students. Often he is complimented by fellow faculty members who say he is "handling" the situation as well as an experienced teacher. With as many as two dozen students who don't want to learn—and who are a constant threat to classroom order— what is Chris to do? So far, there have been enough small successes to keep Chris trying, but his frustration is growing. He doesn't think he could spend a career facing the agonies of educational triage. Who can blame him? He can send one or two of the troublemakers to the principal's office, but as an unwritten rule, if he sends many more, he will be the one in trouble. The principal's office doesn't know what to do with these kids, either.

In an algebra class Chris wants active student involvement—but he has only ten sets of manipulatives, so kids have to share or, more accurately, one will try while the others doze or talk. He uses worksheets a lot, and although he knows that they are not very effective, they create a semblance of order.

We really admire Chris. He is creative and takes initiative. When one student said he didn't have enough time to get from his earlier class to his locker and then to class in the five minutes between bells, Chris walked him through the routine with a stopwatch. The first time he didn't make it, but by the third try, he had it down to three and a half minutes—a minute and a half to spare. The other kids in the class found out about this "drill," and peer pressure has worked—the student hasn't been late since.

Another example is Laura, who has decided to go into gifted education because she finds a greater challenge in teaching kids who want to learn. It is a rational decision, but we lament that this creative teacher won't be helping the kids who need her most.

A third example of the realities that new teachers must face is an Old Dominion graduate named Danny who moved to a university town with "good student demographics." The community is proud of its schools and supports them well—most of them, that is. Danny was attending graduate school at the University of Virginia, and the only job he could find in the area was in the alternative school, the school for those students who do not fit in anywhere else. You would think that with a population of difficult students there would be more resources, but that is not the case. Danny had to teach eight classes a day—in a regular school, teachers expect to teach five classes. His classes are larger than average because the town invited the neighboring school districts to send their alternative kids—without increasing its staff. This was done to recoup some of the costs of the alternative school.

In this situation, Danny wasn't expected to accomplish much. There wasn't a lot of pressure on him so long as he kept the kids occupied. Most of the people involved were simply waiting for the clock to tick long enough for the kids to leave school. But what happens after that?

We know enough to do better in these situations, but the structure of education won't allow it. These teachers don't have either the training or the resources to cope, and neither do those in charge of teacher education. Teacher education is full of suggestions for motivating students, for individualizing instruction, for paying attention to individual needs. No one can dispute the value of that advice. There is lots of evidence that more than 90 percent of all students can learn, and there are abundant success stories to prove that almost all kids can learn. But success stories from the difficult student populations almost always have a kicker. For example, they may involve public schools acting like private schools—kids apply to get in, parents agree to spend time with their kids, and kids can be thrown out if they don't succeed. Suggestions for motivating students, individualizing instruction, and paying attention to individual needs do work when the conditions are right, but the right conditions are rare, usually they are put into practice only in special schools, with additional selection criteria for staff and students, and are impossible to carry out in the vast majority of public schools without the restructuring we propose.

In ordinary public schools, with limited resources, the best we can recommend is a kind of triage: deciding where to spend time to gain the most effect. In Chris's case there is no hope that all thirty-five students will learn—though new external examinations will ultimately try to hold the school and Chris vaguely responsible for their learning. The test scores for the school will be depressed as a result of their failure. To survive, the schools will try to find creative ways to eliminate these students from the test results, tacitly (or even blatantly) encouraging them to be absent on standardized test days, or even encouraging the students to drop out of school entirely.

We can and should teach all the kids—and in general they all can learn. It makes sense to take care of both the learning and behavioral problems of students early. A high school student with eight to ten years of learning deficits may be beyond help. When a student is three years behind in reading performance as a tenth grader, it will take time, patience, and massive resources to do what is necessary to prevent further learning deficits from accumulating.

There are lots of programs geared toward addressing these problems. Perhaps the best example is the Head Start initiative, which has more than proved its worth. But decades later, many eligible students don't have access to these federally subsidized programs. However, even those statistics showing strong success are deceiving, because Head Start students do *better* but they have not received enough help to put them on par with other students. It makes sense to invest in premediation, identifying problems that are likely to occur and developing strategies to keep them from happening—to keep the kids from falling behind. That's many times less expensive and saves the human cost of failure later. But it will require an entirely different level of resources to have any chance of success.

Staff Development:
Ongoing Professional Training

Historically, staff development has never been effective, because staff development cannot be effective in a siege atmosphere. Schools need massive resources, not incremental resources. The question that we must answer is this: How bad will schools have to get before we get serious about fixing them?

The teaching staff needs different preparation—we need to develop experimental teacher-training programs with more classroom experience, more technology training, and a better balance between content and methods preparation. We need to think of the lifelong training of all teachers and administrators. The new concept is that a teacher is never trained, always in training. These programs can be developed in concert with the NESA schools, providing models that can ultimately be made available to all teachers. Internet-based staff development programs are a good start, but must be accompanied by a wide variety of face-to-face programs in the schools.

Teacher-Training Necessities

If we take seriously the task of effectively preparing teachers, we recognize that a few courses in the methods of teaching do not constitute adequate preparation. The idea that they do is absurd. How can we allow the process of teacher education to take fewer resources than the training of doctors and engineers, physicists and lawyers?

We must release teacher training from the paradigm of the three Rs. Don't misunderstand—reading, writing, and arithmetic will remain basic to our success, but they are only the beginning to an educated citizen of the twenty-first century.

Effective teacher training should be very hands-on, with individualized feedback and support, similar to medical internships with their large portions of expensive diagnostic supervision. Although it seems we are constantly citing the costs of these much-needed reforms, we do so not to bemoan them but because it is important that we expect to pay a high price.

It is obvious that society values teaching as a profession, but it doesn't allow the strength of professional training to support it. A three-year professional degree program, with increasing levels of teaching responsibility that culminates in a yearlong paid internship, would transform the profession.

Educational research labs could develop research programs to support various new skills. We need the confidence that there will be time in an expanded teacher preparation program for the mastery of new and complex skills. Hopefully, systematic in-service programs would be developed to retrain in-service teachers to master the same skills.

Teachers as Learners and Learners as Teachers

No longer can teachers be "expert" in all that they teach. In the past teachers learned their subject, learned how to teach

109

it, and then shared their carefully mastered knowledge with successive generations of students. Now there is no teaching subject where the knowledge base is stable. New knowledge is being generated constantly and in some instances exponentially. This means that not only do teachers have to update their knowledge constantly, but also students may have knowledge that the teacher has not yet encountered. School is only one of the places in which to learn. Television, computers, newspapers, magazines, and personal experience are all important sources for new knowledge. The expectation that teachers will always know more than their students is hopelessly outdated. This is as true for elementary students as it is for Ph.D. candidates.

A whole new mindset is required. Teachers have to expect not to know everything and to be comfortable with this fact. Students will routinely learn things outside school and thus have knowledge to share with the teacher. The implications for the teaching/learning process are profound. Typically, teachers are embarrassed if they are "caught" making a mistake in their presentation, have incomplete information, or can't answer a question. On the other hand, students are often embarrassed for the teacher and pretend not to notice mistakes. It is anti-intellectual to encourage students not to share their insights and knowledge with teachers and classmates. Even more debilitating is the requirement that teachers not go beyond the formal curriculum established by the local school board or the state. This dilemma is caused by our wanting standards and accountability. We need to know that our children are being taught and mastering the "right things," which is appropriate. But there needs to be a balance, and teachers should be encouraged to enrich the curriculum by their own experience, to use their own personal examples and styles. Teachers also need to build on the real experiences of their students to make the curriculum come alive and apply basic knowledge to the world around them with confidence.

It is not a simple endeavor to make the curriculum alive and apply basic principles to the world of students. The current process of education is very self-contained. States adopt "standards of learning" to define what teachers should teach and students should learn. This creates the need for standardized testing, which in turn requires teachers to "teach for the test." This generates yet more problems. What does the teacher do when the standards are out of date? With knowledge constantly changing, it is impossible for the participants to remain on the "same page."

Technology for Kids, Teachers, and Schools: The Technology Impact of the $100 Billion Challenge for American Education

We are proposing that almost half the total input of the $100 billion challenge to improve American education be spent on technology and its use.

The big picture is easy: We want every schoolchild and every teacher in America to have a computer linked to the Internet and know how to use it. Every school must have the technology in the school to build systematically on the technological literacy that individual computers at home will make possible. Increasingly, homes will have their own computers, but we propose to lessen the digital divide by providing students with laptop computers that can be used both at home and at school. But allocating the financial resources is only the beginning of the challenge.

Once we make the commitment as a society to achieve this goal, there are many issues to be worked out. For example, how will we distribute computers to the kids, and which computers will we provide? How will we keep track of laptop computers that kids take home and are lost or stolen? The suppliers of such massive technology will make fortunes, and we must try to do a better job of educational procurement than we have done as a nation in the defense industry. That won't be easy. It is vital to set up the means of selection, distribution, and accountability fairly and efficiently. We want to achieve a balance of decentralization with the economies of large-scale purchase.

As we establish a massive technology program for our schools, we must develop sound principles of support. Suppliers should be required to repair and maintain the equipment they sell for the life of the product's intended use as a part of their bid price. Most equipment can simply be swapped for refurbished equipment within twenty-four hours when there are faults or failures. There are already examples of such "in-home warranties" in the marketplace today. Updates and upgrades should also be built in to the program with ongoing technical support. Again, we must try to do better than the military, where support systems for technology have been sporadic, expensive, and often ineffective.

Recycling obsolete equipment must be a part of the program. After exhausting the reasonable potential for updating and upgrading it in place, we must make predictable after-market use of obsolete equipment.

What a wonderful challenge lies ahead for the nation as we embark on a journey to tap the potential of an enlightened citizenry equipped with the power of technology.

Accountability

How do we get the proper accountability in education? It is unreasonable to expect the public to write a blank check for education, and even if we could, educators wouldn't want it. As educators, we feel better when we are accountable. However, there are at least three essential problems with accountability:

1. The community is ambivalent about its goals. This, in turn, makes it impossible for us to know what is expected, let alone how to be accountable.
2. Often the most important objectives of teaching and learning, such as creativity and thinking skills, are difficult, if not impossible, to measure because we lack the right measurement tools.
3. Some of the important objectives of education can be measured only indirectly because their effects can be judged only long after implementation.

The "bottom line" of accountability—student achievement—is the result of so many interacting factors that it is almost impossible to assign individual credit or blame to schools, school administrators, or individual teachers.

113

Our accountability task is much more complex than individual credit or blame. It must become systemic. As we invest the necessary resources to make it reasonable to achieve success under the wide variety of challenges American education faces, broad principles of accountability will emerge, and entire organizations and approaches can be redefined or replaced as necessary. Then it will become more reasonable to exercise rigorous individual accountability as well.

A National Experimental School Administration (NESA)

The Concept of NESA

One of the most visionary and successful, yet controversial, agencies of our time is NASA, the National Aeronautics and Space Administration. Now, in education, we must explore the frontiers just inside the classroom door. These frontiers are as vast as outer space. We must explore new galaxies of curricula and new launch vehicles for teaching, using new telescopes to bring good practices into focus. A national network of experimental schools would give us the power to try out new ideas. It would allow us to get reliable evidence of what works and what doesn't, and determine what practices depend on teachers, communities, and students for their success or failure, and how. We propose the establishment of the National Experimental Schools Administration (NESA).

114

NESA experimental school districts would be formed within current district jurisdictions. An experimental school district would be a single high school and its feeder schools. In Anytown, USA, you wouldn't have all the schools in the experimental school district, just one high school with its feeder schools, which would be exempted from local and state regulations.

There are about 50 million kids in America's public school system, K–12. One percent would be about 500,000 kids. If NESA school districts consisted of a high school feeder pattern that averaged about 5,000 kids, we recommend creating 100 NESA school districts with at least one experimental school district in each state.

Experimental districts would be established in localities that request to be part of the project. This would mean that no community would be required to be part of the NESA network. If you force anyone to take part, they will complain about everything that goes wrong. However when participation is voluntary, when things go wrong it's easier to get everyone to work together to fix it. Let's not fool ourselves into thinking that nothing will go wrong. Inevitably problems will occur, even severe problems like the Challenger disaster in NASA. These problems are all part of the recognized risk of any real experimental efforts. The important thing, which must happen for this system to be successful, must be that when a problem does occur, everyone will pull together to solve it rather than attacking the program or its participants.

NESA districts would develop relationships with local and national universities and with the regional educational laboratories. Both the U.S. Department of Education and state departments of education would contribute to the experimental agenda. Some experimental agendas would be defined within the districts themselves.

Consider one of the most important issues in education: the teaching of reading. There is now broad agreement on the basic principles of reading instruction. There has been general professional consensus for years that phonics is an important aid to learning. Phonics doesn't link words to meanings, however, and that's where "whole language" comes in. It's pretty obvious that just being able to sound out words doesn't get the job done. However well you can decipher sounds and symbols, you still need meaning. Those involved in this argument have been virtually at war with each other over which method of reading education to use, when the responsible answer is to use both—phonics early, and whole language learning soon after.

Some want only phonics, some want only whole language, and kids become the victims in such games because they don't get the reading instruction they need. The media has overblown the argument, which has been fueled by the rhetoric of zealots on all sides. The issue is further complicated by the fact that there is much money to be made in selling reading materials, and many careers are based on advocacy of these approaches. We need a neutral outside source to arbitrate this discussion and to conduct further research.

America needs an impartial source of information about education, where the merits of all points of view are reasonably represented. NESA would serve as a clearinghouse for our knowledge about educational practice. NESA schools would become frontiers for educational change. The challenge is to establish NESA with impartial credibility and without a vast educational bureaucracy. We can never be sure that NESA could prove immune from the factionalism that plagues education today, but we all win, as the American people, if we can build the common will to succeed.

Initially, NESA's experimental programs would affect only its own schools. However, the implications are clear. When they succeed in NESA, programs and methods should be considered for general school adoption. The decision of what to adopt from NESA would remain a local or state decision.

Organization of NESA

Local Experimental School Districts

Communities would have to apply for admittance into NESA. We anticipate a high level of interest and competition to receive a NESA grant. Communities would discuss the pros and cons of being a NESA school district and decide whether or not they wanted to participate. There will be numerous benefits for NESA communities:

- excitement of participating in new educational concepts
- state-of-the-art schools

117

- close evaluation of schools, programs, and individual success
- a commitment to remediate unsuccessful students in NESA programs
- new jobs in the community
- an impartial review panel would be convened to make NESA district selections

We propose that a community be required to make a twenty-year commitment when bidding to become a NESA school district. And NESA would make a similar twenty-year commitment to the community. One of the reasons a long-term commitment is required is that NESA will provide buildings to house experimental staff for a long-term program. We are looking for communities that recognize the challenge and joy of being part of a new and important educational experience.

The interface with the regular schools is very important to the NESA concept. Every district would be matched to a regular district, and students would be allowed to attend the alternative district if they wished. In the NESA program, transportation to the closest nonexperimental school would be provided at NESA cost, so parents and kids would have a genuine, nonpunitive choice. We want the people who are in a NESA system to want to be there. Students in the matched school district can be given opportunities to fill the spaces that any transfers create, and transportation would be provided for them as well.

National Coordination of NESA

An individual should not head NESA. Instead, a small group (nine to twelve people) modeled after the Supreme Court should head this organization. It's unrealistic to think that we can keep politics out of it, but at least we can minimize the effects. The governing charter would include guidelines to promote geographic, gender, and ethnic diversity. There should be a balance of persons from urban and rural backgrounds.

Term lengths would be set appropriately depending on the size of this group. A nine-person board might have each member serve for one nine-year, nonrenewable term. Each year, one member would be appointed to lessen the partisan political leverage. A twelve-person board could have members serve six-year terms, with the possibility of one renewal. Each year two positions would be up for appointment or reappointment.

It is important for NESA to transcend partisan politics. We lose as a society if we checkmate ourselves by seeking narrow political advantage. It is hard enough to make schools work and educate the bottom quartile of kids, without complicating the issues with political maneuvering.

The NESA board would oversee the $5 billion NESA budget, but without a large bureaucracy. Most national NESA initiatives would be subcontracted to agencies and organizations, public and private, but the heart of the NESA program would be the network of one hundred experimental school districts with direct funding.

Funding NESA Districts

NESA funding will cover the evaluation cost of experiments, the development of curricula, and the transfers and transport of reluctant teachers and students. Funds would not be spent on the ordinary recurrent costs of a NESA school, which will come from the same sources and in the same amounts as other local schools.

If experimental schools can figure out how to do a better job within the boundaries of regular resources, then we will have the most persuasive model to follow. Initially, that's the place to start. Give experimental schools not a lot more than the same regular operating funding as the school next door. However, substantial additional funding will be provided for research, development and evaluation, and remediation. The added experimental resources should probably double the regular resources, and the experimental staff may well equal the regular staff. As we have said, experimentation and evaluation are expensive. It doesn't cost more to teach a new curriculum once it is developed, but it requires money to develop that new curriculum. It takes time and energy, as well as additional computer materials, video materials, and textbooks to support it. These must be funded by NESA.

With one hundred districts developing in part on their own, in part as a national network, we can amass a body of knowledge about the experimental process. There are new subjects to be considered and alternative ways to present curriculum—in interdisciplinary settings, in projects, or in yet-to-be-developed ways that apply knowledge in a practical way. We need to investigate new patterns of schooling, some requiring or offering more time in schools, some with the same number of days spread throughout the year. We need to experiment with school schedules that offer programs in the evenings and on weekends, and options where students and teachers arrive and depart individually rather than all at once. Some teachers may arrive at 7:00 A.M., and leave at 3:00 P.M., others may come at noon and leave at 8:00 P.M. The same flexibility could be built in for students. In the past some school districts have had double schedules, with completely different morning and afternoon schools. This is not what we have in mind. Some of these patterns will cost more, some merely will allocate time and resources differently. But all will require extensive resources to determine their effectiveness and consequences.

In addition, we'd like to develop a computerized testing program. We would like to know how people who take quizzes with computers perform against those who don't. We would like to see how attitudes toward testing compare, and if there are differences in the amount of cheating. We would like to know if there are students and groups of students who are less able to perform well in a computer-testing environment.

To finance a hundred NESA schools, with the national coordination to support them, we propose an initial budget of about $4 billion a year (of the $5 billion total NESA budget) to fund national, regional, and local experimental programs, and to provide technology and other special equipment. That figure sounds large, but it is well within our resources as a nation, a modest investment to transform our educational system to meet twenty-first century needs, an issue of national security.

This would provide a budget of about $30 million per NESA school. About half of that would be administered at a local level—in direct support for each school. The other half would fund developmental costs for curricula and for curriculum materials (including computer software) and the development of new equipment and technologies, and would support national research and evaluation costs.

We suggest an experimental operating budget of $3,000 per student annually to begin. This would provide funds for a substantial program of experimentation. With NESA districts averaging about five thousand students each, an annual operating budget (staff and facility) of about $15 million per district would be appropriate at the beginning. As we go along, we will undoubtedly identify new experimental requirements and thus we might expect the budget for experimentation to grow to equal the average current per-pupil expenditure—that would be an estimated $25 million per year per NESA district. As NESA schools begin to produce results, we will become more enthusiastic about increasing their resources. Among the first priorities is to create a research facility for each local NESA school district. We estimate that about $2 million per district would be required to build this facility. With a twenty-year commitment, facilities would be built with bonds and amortized over the twenty-year life of the project. Some projects might require modification of the basic school facilities as well, and funding should be available for this purpose as needed.

There is general agreement that we need a strong technology initiative in our schools. We suggest that a billion dollars per year be invested in the one hundred NESA districts for technology program development. That breaks down to another $10 million per district per year. About half of this would be spent nationally for development.

A $5-billion-per-year investment in one hundred NESA schools may seem like a large amount, but take into account that the total investment in public K–12 education per year is about $200 billion (47 percent of which comes from local property taxes, 47 percent from the state, and about 6 percent from the federal government). With those numbers in mind, it becomes easier to envision an investment of about 2.5 percent of the total being put toward the development of a NESA school network. Education has to be thought of as a part of the larger society, which is rapidly changing, requiring ever-increasing investment in research and development.

There is general agreement about the need, but little confidence about the educational system's ability to deliver. A well-funded NESA will provide no guarantees, and NESA could fail; but more likely, with constant redefinition for at least two decades, NESA has an excellent chance for success. The alternative we face is immobilization, further decay, and despair about the ultimate success of our nation's schools.

NESA Guidelines

The mandate of the NESA school network would call for funding of local, state, and national experimental initiatives. In our proposal, approximately half of all experiments would be part of a coordinated national program, a quarter would be state or regional, and a quarter would be local initiatives in each NESA school—all funded by NESA. In other words, in each local NESA school district, one quarter of its national funding would fund experimental programs of the school's own design. Thus we would leverage the genius of the American way and combine the benefits of large-scale initiatives and local adaptations.

A twenty-year mandate is necessary to sustain NESA schools. In the past, anytime the wind blew, someone would get mad and pull the plug. A NESA school must continue even if it is unpopular. The popular thing to do is not always the right thing to do. More important is maintaining continuity in experimentation to gain confident perspectives of what works and why and how for the education of our children.

Even if the experiment does not reach its full potential, we learn from the mistakes we make, and by correcting them, we improve. The NESA national school board would direct the national experimentation and the NESA local board would administer national initiatives and develop and manage local experimentation.

NESA's mandate would be to develop the broadest national consensus for action. It is important to decide where local, regional, and national actions are appropriate.

Staff would develop and circulate "working papers" to receive feedback on various issues. Local, state, and regional hearings would then be held in order to tabulate public responses. This would in effect be a structured "straw vote."

This process must not be hurried, but it should move forward on a set timetable. It will take time to develop the infrastructure so the process flows easily, but once that is done, people will start to realize that their voices count. And since the NESA school system will develop close relationships with the existing national education laboratories and local universities, funding can be provided for joint initiatives.

We want people at the experimental schools—students, teachers, administrators, and experimental staff—who want to be there and who understand both the risks and the opportunities. We are confident that we can find communities that are willing to support dramatic and large-scale initiatives for educational change. And we will provide access to conventional schools for any families who choose not to participate.

NESA Relationships with Local Universities and Regional Education Laboratories

It would be unfair to imply that the proposal for systematic research in education is new. For decades the U.S. Department of Education and its predecessor, the U.S. Office of Education, have funded Regional Educational Laboratories that have made substantial contributions to almost all the areas we propose to fund. But they have not had the resources to undertake systemic reform, to put together initiatives of the magnitude that is required if we are to address such pervasive issues as the restructuring of the entire teaching profession. The Regional Education Laboratories have undertaken significant research and development in education, but they have often been isolated from the mainstream without predictable sites for their research. And their findings have not had a systematic opportunity for application. By linking Regional Educational Laboratories to NESA school districts, their potential will be greatly increased. They will work with NESA schools as partners. They will also become likely agencies to bid on national NESA initiatives, along with other public and private agencies.

Local universities will be expected to develop close relationships with NESA schools. Some NESA school experimental staff may have joint appointments with local universities. Teacher training and staff development will be a natural component of NESA programs, and the cooperation of colleges and universities is essential. There will be a crucial difference, however. In the past, universities have come to schools with programs in mind, inviting school districts to participate. In NESA schools, the schools will become full partners with universities in the development of experimental initiatives.

Challenges Facing Experimental Schools

Trust

There are many problems in education, trust being the biggest. We are quick to blame and slow to trust. We have to trust each other as we all make mistakes, and learn to celebrate "good mistakes" from which we learn. Somehow we have to combat the jealousy of success which so often cripples experimental efforts. If we are going to have successful NESA schools, we will have to develop behaviors that lead to trust, including a high tolerance for risk and error. Local and national NESA school boards must be as impartial as possible, above partisanship and self-interest. We must take great care in setting up selection processes for NESA school districts that the public can have confidence in. Getting school populations that are representative is tough: we need to have rural and urban populations, and multiethnic populations, as well as ways of balancing the geographical representation of NESA schools. If we don't have a representative population, then we will not be able to apply the results predictably when we have learned what initiatives are successful. We must have reason to trust that NESA schools will represent everyone and are designed to produce successful and appropriate school programs for all students, not just those headed for college as has been typical of schools in the past.

Defining the Experimental Agenda

The most important question for any researcher is: What issue do I study? If we study issues that are simply refinements of past practice, we are perpetuating a system that we already know is not functioning well and is not able to use new technologies and resources that are available. We must define experimental agendas that are bold, try out alternatives, and go beyond what we have tried in the past. True experimental agendas are inherently risky, and having the safety net of NESA will make much more far-reaching experimentation possible.

This situation shows that we are not spending enough on education now, so if we say we can't spend more on the operational budgets of the experimental schools, then we may be precluded from trying important alternatives. As separate initiatives we are proposing dramatic increases in expenditure for teacher salaries and to bolster teacher education. We'll have to constantly reexamine our positions and alternatives as time passes. Even though we say the experimental schools will have enough resources and be exempt from most regulatory input, it will not be easy to balance realistic agendas with well-understood educational needs. NESA schools will be designed to be independent, but they won't be able to use this freedom fully if they don't feel the support and confidence of the society.

Accountability

Making NESA schools independent of regulatory authority does not mean that they should not be accountable. It is important, however, that they are not simply perceived as accountable but, rather, actually are accountable. The local NESA boards should be accountable to the staff, parents, and communities they serve. The national NESA board should be very open in its mode of operation and demonstrate its accountability by regularly seeking input from the profession and the citizenry through open forums, with open meetings and transparent decision making, and effective dissemination of information about the successes and failures of its programs. Experimental initiatives should be thoroughly explained. It is particularly important to report and document failures. The way failure and problems are handled will to a large extent determine the confidence level of the public in NESA schools.

Evaluation and Implementation

It is going to be tough to evaluate the programs to find out what works and why, and ultimately it is going to be tougher to apply these lessons to the regular schools. NESA will have to keep the public well informed about all its initiatives, on both local and national levels. Evaluation of all NESA initiatives must be open, transparent, and invite public scrutiny. This will require NESA researchers to develop new strategies for the design and reporting of experimental programs. The NESA experimental school system will not solve all our problems, but if we can make a start, we can expect to find new approaches along the way.

Private-sector support to NESA will also be crucial for its success. Some of this support can be pro bono—community investment. But the private sector can also offer resources for research and development, and join forces with NESA researchers to develop new technologies and find new ways to use existing technologies in the schools. The private sector can help define and develop curriculum which is consistent with its needs, and make available from its own vast training resources expertise, materials, and programs which can be modified for school use. It should be routine for private and other public sector employees to be encouraged to volunteer, on company time, to assist in the schools. These goods and services should not be limited to NESA schools, of course, but this would be an excellent milieu in which to develop models and patterns for such support.

If all goes well, school districts around the nation will turn to NESA for guidance on what programs to consider and why. If all goes well, the American public will finally have a confident mechanism for accountability as our national defense shield of education becomes stronger and as we reach for new levels of global interdependence.

PART 3
The Costs Involved

$100 Billion a Year for Education—Summary

18 Ways—BIT by BIT★ to Start to Transform American Schools

★BIT—Billion-dollar Initiative for Transformation

Teachers: $35 Billion

$6 billion: Regular in-service training on the Internet for all teachers.

Compensate every teacher in America $2,000 per year to spend two hours a week on the Internet upgrading knowledge of his or her subjects, teaching methods, and of the newest research.

$2 billion: A trained corps of master teacher mentors.

Provide a trained corps of clinical master teacher mentors for each teacher in training and for beginning teachers.

$5 billion: A corps of $100,000 classroom teachers.

Pay 5 percent of all teachers an added $50,000 per year to attract and hold a share of the brightest college and university graduates as master teachers.

$10 billion: Teaching assistants and other support staff for teachers.

Build the concept of "the teacher and his or her staff" with clerical and technical support in the classroom, including teaching assistants and interns.

$1 billion: Challenge grants for teacher initiatives for educational reform.

Teachers should be encouraged to examine their own practices and to try new initiatives. A series of challenge grants should be established, with teachers from other states making the judgment about the priorities of which initiatives to fund.

$6 billion: Six years of pre-service training for teachers.

Provide $10,000 per year for six years of university teacher training for 100,000 teachers each year.

$3 billion: One-year internships for teachers after professional training.

Provide $30,000 per teacher to support one-year internships for 100,000 teachers in training each year

$1 billion: Higher salaries for more teacher educators.

Increase the salaries of 10,000 teacher educators by $25,000 to $75,000 per year to attract a share of the brightest graduates to teacher education, and hire more teacher educators and researchers in colleges of education.

$1 billion: Development of teacher-training materials.

Pay for the development of a rich curriculum of Internet pre-service and in-service teacher education in one-hour modules.

Technology: $32 Billion

$15 billion: Technology for all schools—purchase, maintenance, and replacement.

Equip all schools with multimedia technology, including computers connected to the Internet with funding for systematic replacement on a five-year cycle.

$15 billion: A laptop or home computer for every student, connected to the Internet.

We must solve the problem of overcoming the digital divide. Provide every schoolchild in America with either a laptop computer that can be used at home and at school, or a home computer connected to the Internet with replacement every three years.

$2 billion: A computer at home for every teacher, connected to the Internet.

Provide every teacher with a computer at home connected to the Internet and replace it every three years.

Curriculum: $6 Billion

$6 billion: Continuous curriculum development for all subjects with Internet support.

Continuous curriculum development for all subjects with Internet support.

Organization: $20 Billion

$5 billion: Year-round schooling.

The evidence is building for the importance of year-round schooling. Let us begin by funding a wide array of year-round schools for communities that choose to participate, and keep a close watch on the results.

$10 billion: Extended day schooling.

Provide extended day schooling and care to keep all our kids off the streets until their parents get home.

$5 billion: Alternative schools for all levels of education.

Support the development of alternative schools at all levels of education. School choice will provide parents more voice in the education of their kids.

Accountability: $7 Billion

$2 billion: Ongoing evaluation of current school practice.

Develop broad programs of evaluation to examine systematically the wealth of experience in current educational practice, building on the current excellent but limited efforts of the U.S. Department of Education.

$5 billion: NESA, a national experimental school system.

Establish a national experimental school system with one hundred semiautonomous local experimental school districts, preschool through the twelfth grade, to systematically test local and national alternatives to find out what really works—why and how.

$100 Billion for Education—Further Elaboration

Teachers: $35 Billion

$6 billion: Regular in-service training on the Internet for all teachers.

Compensate every teacher in America $2,000 per year to spend two hours a week on the Internet upgrading knowledge of his or her subjects, teaching methods, and of the newest research.

We all agree that lots of teachers are out of date in their knowledge of both content and method of teaching practice. Current methods are hit and miss and often not valued by the teachers who receive such training. The Internet offers a dramatic new potential. Developing and presenting new content and methods in a systematic way for all teachers can now be routine and cost-effective in a way never before possible.

We could offer every teacher in America $20 per hour for up to two hours a week to participate in in-service teacher education on the Internet to keep up with new knowledge and methods—about $2,000 per year as long as they are teaching. The top 20 percent of the teachers—identified locally—would be paid $30 per hour as evaluators of training materials.

Avoiding Bureaucracy—A Model for Teacher On-Line Staff Development Program (TOLS)

An Example of National Coordination with Local Implementation and Responsibility

As we develop on-line resources for staff development, it is important to build in opportunities for quality control, assessment, and validation without creating a massive bureaucracy. Fortunately the new technologies surrounding the Internet make that easier. It is unlikely that we will be able to come up with the "ideal" plan at the beginning, but there are many ways to begin to test good strategies. We can be bold in our development strategies.

How might the TOLS Program be managed?

A TOLS Board could be appointed by the U.S. Secretary of Education or by the National Experimental Schools Administration. This twelve- to-fifteen-member board will manage the program. They will need minimum staff, as most of their work will be contracted.

How will TOLS be delivered?

The TOLS Board will develop RFPs (Requests for Proposals) for the development, management, and hosting of TOLS Curriculum materials. Public and private entities will be able to submit bids for the development and management of each TOLS Network.

TOLS Networks will not have responsibility for validating or evaluating materials. Their only responsibility will be to host materials from accredited agencies and to account for and report program usage.

It is anticipated that two or three TOLS Networks will be established, operating independently to provide multiple perspectives on training success. Initially all curriculum developers will be randomly assigned to one of these networks. After a year or two, criteria for participation in different networks may be developed by the TOLS Board, and networks and developers will be encouraged to establish special arrangements.

Who is eligible to take training?

All full-time teachers in public school districts will be eligible. Public school districts will be eligible to register with the TOLS Program. Each registered school district will provide all full-time teachers with TOLS ID numbers. School districts will receive monthly reports of TOLS participation by their staff members from the TOLS Networks. School districts will pay teachers for TOLS Program participation after receiving verification of teacher participation and will add

TOLS payment to teachers' salary checks. School districts will be reimbursed by the National TOLS Board. Private schools will be invited to use TOLS materials to train their teachers and pay a users fee. Compensation for private schoolteachers will be arranged by the private schools themselves.

Who will develop TOLS materials?

All professional educational associations and organizations will be eligible to produce materials. Each organization will be accredited by the National TOLS Board and assigned to a TOLS development level according to its membership rolls. The higher the level of accreditation, the more materials can be developed. Organizations will be paid a standard stipend, perhaps $10,000 per curriculum hour developed. Materials will be developed to fit curriculum templates established by each TOLS Network. In addition to "basic materials" whose content and scope are at the discretion of each developer, the National TOLS Board will develop competitive RFPs for specific materials to meet identified needs. Compensation for such materials may be at a different rate than for basic materials.

How will training materials be validated and evaluated?

Each school district, at its discretion, will be encouraged to designate 20 percent of TOLS-eligible staff as Curriculum Validators. These senior staff will be responsible for the validation of on-line staff development training modules. They will be paid a $10-per-hour premium as validators to evaluate the curriculum materials they complete as a part of their own in-service training. Their evaluations will be immediately tabulated and posted on site as a guide for future participants in choosing their study materials.

Every year, cutoff points will be established, and materials reviewed below acceptable levels of quality will be removed from the TOLS networks. Teachers will be required to complete ever-increasing portions of their training from validated materials.

Agencies developing materials will be given increased or decreased funding for further curriculum development depending on the cumulative evaluation of their materials by the TOLS Curriculum Validators.

In this way, materials will constantly be reviewed and evaluated, and agencies will be encouraged to revise and update their offerings based on evaluative feedback. All of this will be done without creating bureaucratic structures, and is designed to stimulate creativity from the profession as a whole. It has the potential to be dynamic and self-correcting, based on principles of a learning organization.

Our teacher corps will be transformed. Such a program would unleash the creativity of providers who would jump at the opportunity to develop a wide variety of training materials. Funding must also be provided to monitor and evaluate the results, constantly upgrade the quality of training, and find out how best to supplement Internet teacher training with collaborative, in-school training as well.

$2 billion: A trained corps of master teacher mentors.

Provide a trained corps of clinical master teacher mentors for each teacher in training and for beginning teachers.

There would be several important concomitant benefits of paying mentor teachers $2,000-to-$5,000 stipends each year. First of all, well-trained mentors would provide better supervision and guidance for new teachers, and if mentors are well paid, they will be encouraged to provide more and better assistance. Second, this will improve the compensation of master teachers and provide at least modest additional financial incentives for them to stay in the classroom. Also, such mentor teachers could be used to help overcome the existing isolation of teachers generally and encourage teachers to visit each other's classes. Cooperating teachers who now supervise student teachers are rarely trained and are usually compensated as little as $50 per student teacher, and sometimes nothing. Developing a corps of master teacher mentors for teachers in training and beginning teachers is an obvious strategy for the improvement of the profession.

$5 billion: A corps of $100,000 classroom teachers.

Pay 5 percent of all teachers an added $50,000 per year to attract and hold a share of the brightest college and university graduates as master teachers.

We need to break the mold of the single salary schedule for all teachers. Just as the dream of an NBA million-dollar contract energizes sand lot and schoolyard basketball all over the nation, the realistic aspiration for $100,000 stipends per year for even a small percentage of teachers will energize applicants at all levels and increase the recruitment pool. It will take a massive investment to change the image of the profession and allow it to assume parity with other senior professions. It will force schools to think about how to best use their outstanding teachers to make sure that they influence the lives of the most kids. The master teacher stipends should be reserved for professional teachers who spend a minimum of three hours a day in the classroom—not for administrators who have no direct contact with kids. We will send an important message to the profession when the top teachers earn more than the senior school administrators. Eventually all teacher salaries should be substantially improved to make teaching a full-time profession, but it is most important to start at the top, to attract and hold the highest quality teachers.

We expect to have a learning curve. In the beginning the appointment of master teachers by local school districts using locally developed criteria may be flawed in many ways, with little added benefit from the use of master teachers. But as school districts think through how to use this precious resource, local creativity will begin to take hold, and we are confident that new models will emerge for the appointment, training, and use of master teachers.

$10 billion: Teaching assistants and other support staff for teachers.

Build the concept of "the teacher and his or her staff" with clerical and technical support in the classroom, including teaching assistants and interns.

Teachers are now required to "do it all." Teachers are self-contained in their classrooms. Sporadically they may have teaching assistants or some volunteer support. If we are to make the most efficient use of our most valuable resource in education—well-trained teachers—we must begin to provide them the support that is routine for almost all other professionals.

Teachers should have clerical support to run off copies of materials, keep records, and help communicate with parents; technical support to help with mediated presentations and to provide technical support of computers and other equipment in the classroom; and semiprofessional support for tutoring, test monitoring, and other quasi-professional tasks.

We must begin to treat teachers like professionals, not like semiprofessional technicians, which is now standard practice. It will take some time for teachers to learn how to use such professional support, and we must be prepared to invest substantial funds to explore differing staffing options and the training necessary for teachers to fully use such support.

$1 billion: Challenge grants for teacher initiatives for educational reform.

Teachers should be encouraged to examine their own practices and to try new initiatives. A series of challenge grants should be established, with teachers from other states making the judgment about the priorities of which initiatives to fund.

These grants would range from $5,000 to $25,000 and offer the opportunity for creative teachers to try out their own innovative ideas. By having the top teachers, taken from the ranks of TOLS evaluators and master teachers from nearby states, serve on boards to review and approve applications of fellow teachers, we avoid the necessity of creating a centralized bureaucracy to administer the program.

$6 billion: Six years of pre-service training for teachers.

Provide $10,000 per year for six years of university teacher training for 100,000 teachers each year.

There is a wide consensus that we need to attract a share of the brightest students to the profession of teaching. We propose six years of funding as an incentive to increase the time of training and to raise the standards of the teaching profession generally. There are all sorts of variations possible. For example, funding can be in the form of loans that include one year of funding forgiven for every year as a teacher. Some states already have programs that resemble this, with some success. The key will be the simultaneous adoption of a variety of initiatives designed to attract and hold outstanding teachers.

$3 billion: One-year internships for teachers after professional training.

Provide $30,000 per teacher to support one-year internships for 100,000 teachers in training each year.

After six years of college and university training, a compulsory funded internship should provide the transition to professional service. There is consistent agreement by teachers in training that more clinical experience is needed. Providing interns with a $30,000 stipend during an internship year would have many benefits. First, the quality of training would be immediately improved with a yearlong internship experience, compared with current student teaching requirements, which can be as little as six weeks of full-time teaching. Second, interns would provide real additional assistance in schools, and internship positions could be targeted for schools with the greatest need. Third, yearlong internships would encourage stronger links between teacher-training institutions and the schools, a long-recognized weakness of teacher training. Finally, this could begin closing the gap in training levels between education and other professions. This should be a part of a comprehensive effort to make teaching a full-time profession, well enough compensated so our children's educators need not moonlight in second and sometimes even third jobs.

$1 billion: Higher salaries for more teacher educators.

Increase the salaries of 10,000 teacher educators by $25,000 to $75,000 per year to attract a share of the brightest graduates to teacher education, and hire more teacher educators and researchers.

Currently the talent base for the entire profession of teaching is weak. Top candidates are not attracted to the profession, neither as teachers nor as teacher educators. If the society wants to have premium preparation for teachers, the cadre of teacher educators must be upgraded. This will take time, but making available substantial salary premiums for teacher education will, over time, attract a different level of candidate to the profession of teacher education. It is a signal from society that teacher education is a premium endeavor. Currently teacher education programs in colleges and universities are funded at substantially lower levels per student than for engineers, for example.

In addition, we need to increase the number of teacher educators to allow more clinical supervision and closer relationships with schools and to systematically increase the research potential of colleges of education.

$1 billion: Development of teacher-training materials.
Pay for the development of a rich curriculum of Internet pre-service and in-service teacher education in one-hour modules.

When we make a commitment to the ongoing education of teachers, we will be required to rethink the whole process of teacher education. Many of the materials prepared to update the skills of experienced teachers will also be appropriate for pre-service education and will bring much-needed new approaches to teacher education generally. Funding should be provided for material development, experimental training protocols, and the monitoring and evaluation of the effects of training. Pre-service teacher training programs should also be encouraged to use TOLS materials to help teachers in training develop self-instructional training habits which can last for a lifetime of professional service.

Technology: $32 Billion

$15 billion: Technology for all schools—purchase, maintenance, and replacement.
Equip all schools with multimedia technology, including com-

puters connected to the Internet with funding for systematic replacement on a five-year cycle.

Schools will need multimedia technology, including computers connected to the Internet, CD-ROM libraries, television conferencing and satellite connections for distance education, and other technologies just now being developed. We must provide funding for systematic replacement on a five-year cycle.

All over America schools are struggling to find the finances to purchase needed technology—and to upgrade and replace obsolete technology. Most schools are still struggling to acquire necessary equipment, let alone provide adequate budgets to maintain and replace equipment as needed. This program must also be designed to fund technical support for both maintenance and use of the equipment. A whole new category of support personnel must be added to the staffing tables of schools if technology is to achieve its real potential.

$15 billion: A laptop computer for every student, connected to the Internet.

We must solve the problem of overcoming the digital divide. Provide every schoolchild in America with either a laptop computer which can be used at home and at school, or a home computer connected to the Internet with replacement every three years.

Children from poor families must not be left out of the technological age, left on the wrong side of the digital divide. Computers have arrived as an effective tool for education. Stores are filled with educational computer programs for enrichment. But they remain out of reach for the kids who need them most. Schools do not have the money to buy the computers—or software programs—and they don't have the resources to train the teachers to use them. We talk about putting schools on the information highway, and then only dribble funds in that direction. We can easily make our society a computer-literate society, from the poorest kid on up. Already we are seeing a crunch in the private sector—not enough people to compete for the increasing number of high-tech jobs that are multiplying each day. Let's think ahead and make a laptop computer a part of the educational bag for each student. It is already happening in a few schools.

We don't know what to do with such high-tech kids, how to teach them—or even what to teach—but we can learn fast. Create the potential and rely on the creativity of the private and public sectors working together to respond to the opportunities. The name of any state capital or any other factual information is only a few mouse clicks away from any kid connected to the Internet with the skills to use it. Think how the expectations of education can be transformed with laptop computers in the school backpacks of America.

And by the time we can make a computer in the backpack of every kid a reality, the prices will probably be less than half what they are today. Think of all the other needs that we can address with the money we will save!

$2 billion: A computer at home for every teacher, connected to the Internet.

Provide every teacher with a computer at home connected to the Internet and replace it every three years.

It doesn't do any good to give kids computers and leave their teachers behind. Computers should be a routine part of the professional equipment of every teacher. All teachers do much of their work at home and should be provided with the professional equipment to work efficiently. Laptops and Internet connections should be the common professional standard. As a society we cannot afford to have a single teacher who is not up to date in her or his personal access to information and technology.

Curriculum: $6 Billion

$6 billion: Continuous curriculum development for all subjects with Internet support.

All students study the core courses in the curriculum. Gradually we are developing national standards within each subject. The development of on-line support materials does not have to wait for agreement on individual curriculum elements. If we design support materials that are self-contained for each unit or topic, schools and teachers can decide which materials to use and how they will use them. But having support and remedial materials available to all students—who can have access to them at school and at home if we provide every student with a computer—will give teachers substantial new strategies to assist students to keep up and find success in their studies. We must invest time and resources to develop the materials, train teachers how to use them, develop easy access to the materials, provide support for interactive student participation and feed-back, and keep records of student participation and success in using the materials.

The "other subjects," such as the arts, vocational educa-tion, and physical education, also need support materials. Fundamentally they are as important as the core subjects. Who can argue about the importance of health and fitness, of the value of the aesthetic quality of life and widespread community appreciation for and participation in the arts? Our commitment as a society to nonacademic subjects such as vocational education has been very spotty, to the detri-ment of a large group of students who will not go on to college and university. Providing Internet support materials for nonacademic subjects will be more difficult since there is less agreement on curriculum elements, but we must invest in alternatives and gradually shape multiple curricula to enrich the total quality of our educational experience and provide better education for all students.

Organization: $20 Billion

$5 billion: Year-round schooling.

The evidence is building for the importance of year-round school-ing, but many communities are not yet ready for it, and don't have the local resources to fund it. Let us begin by funding a wide array of year-round schools for communities who choose to participate, and keep a close watch on the results.

We must be prepared to fund some version of year-round schooling for all students within a generation. Some year-round efforts have not been successful in the past. Many have been successful and continue. We must learn to distinguish between sound initiatives implemented unsuccessfully and ill-conceived programs. This is a vivid example of how a completely new mind-set, along with dramatic increases in resources, will be required to make education really functional in the new millennium. Different models can be funded in local communities willing to experiment with year-round schooling.

$10 billion: Extended day schooling.
Provide extended day schooling and care to keep all our kids off the streets until their parents get home.

As a society we are just beginning to realize the social costs of having our kids go home to empty houses after school with no supervision. We can no longer predict that individual families will be able to provide supervision of children in the afternoon. Extended day schooling may be primarily motivated by the need for supervision, but it will provide for an entirely new array of opportunities. Students can have systematic access to tutoring. Extended days provide a rich opportunity for remediation as needed. Enrichment and elective subjects can be added. The extracurriculum will be energized. The arts will have new opportunities for participation and appreciation. Physical fitness can be developed in ways to build lifetime habits of regular exercise, which we now know contributes to both mental and physical well-being. And if both students and teachers can complete homework before dinner, we restore a whole new potential for extended family interaction in the evenings.

$5 billion: Alternative schools for all levels of education.

Support the development of alternative schools at all levels of education. School choice will provide parents more voice in the education of their kids.

America became great because this is the land of choice and opportunity. There is a real grassroots effort to diversify our education. Alternative schools should be encouraged and funded—but not as a disguised way of avoiding diversity or further segregating our kids and leaving behind the disadvantaged kids with no one to speak for them.

Many alternatives can be developed within existing structures and facilities—schools within schools. Communities can be encouraged and funded to turn over selected public school facilities to alternative schools under private, nonprofit sponsorship allowing for the teaching of controversial subjects, alternative schedules, and innovative staffing arrangements. There are already prototypes of charter schools. This initiative could begin with a series of local and regional alternative schools conferences to make sure that all voices are heard and that educational choice becomes a building block for common future educational alternatives. We must invest in alternatives and, equally important, invest in monitoring and evaluating the success and failure of these alternatives.

The difference between funding alternative schools and providing vouchers is the difference between providing a hunting license and something to hunt. Any voucher system which provides less than the full cost of education will be necessarily skewed in favor of those families which can afford to make up the difference.

Vouchers that are offered to students in schools which are identified as less than successful also miss the point. Choice and alternatives are needed for the individual students who fail—and there are students in schools which are successful by any accountability criteria or testing program who are not successful. We believe that these kids can often be reached by providing alternatives—either within the current schools or in alternative schools or programs. When schools fail, the schools should be treated, taken over, supplemented, or restaffed. When individuals fail, whether their school is successful or unsuccessful, they need personal access to new approaches, supplementary programs, or alternative schools. Can we be creative enough to create responsible, accountable alternatives without a massive bureaucracy to oversee them at either the national or state level? It's worth more than $5 billion to find out.

Accountability: $7 Billion

$2 Billion: Ongoing evaluation of current school practice.

Develop broad programs of evaluation to examine systematically the wealth of experience in current educational practice, building on the current excellent but limited efforts of the U.S. Department of Education.

$5 billion: NESA, a national experimental school system.

Establish a national experimental school system to systematically test alternatives and find out what really works—why and how.

We desperately need to have a predictable way to test

what works and what doesn't. A national network of experimental schools should operate with resources that will make it possible for other schools to adopt their successful initiatives without massive additional funding. The key will be to provide sufficient resources to allow systematic testing and evaluation of new practices under diverse conditions, short term and long term, so that we learn what works and why. Too much educational practice is now driven either by tradition or intuition. We simply don't have the sites or the resources to systematically test and evaluate substantial alternatives. Serious experimentation requires mounting and testing alternatives. It requires trial and error. It requires the provision for remediation when experiments fail.

Education has never had a very large R&D budget. A few years ago, someone estimated that the entire R&D budget for education would build only two feet of an aircraft carrier each year. At that rate it would take more than four hundred years to build an aircraft carrier! It doesn't make sense not to invest more systematically in a system of experimental schools and transform the roles of current regional education laboratories to support them.

You Can Help Us Begin

It is hard to anticipate what the true costs of educational transformation will be. And it is certain that many mistakes will be made along the way. We have only to recall the $750 coffeepots and billions of dollars invested in tanks that never performed satisfactorily to know that national security is costly and not error free.

We offer a series of specific proposals, with estimates of their initial cost, in order to share our vision of what is possible, bit by bit. We are not suggesting that these are the only proposals to be considered, or that they will not require further refinement. But we want to give enough specifics to create a vision of what is possible. Education can be used to reduce welfare rolls, to help kids learn that violence is not a good solution for any problem, to help reshape the eating and exercise practices of a nation jeopardized by its unhealthy practices, to take advantage of what we have learned from a myriad of research. Education can contribute substantially to the physical and mental health of the nation.

The heart of the matter is to reshape the teaching profession, to recruit and retain our share of the brightest students and train them well. We need to examine the cost implications of a commitment to technology and its effective use. We must try new organizational patterns, to escape the obsolete school schedules designed for a rural, agricultural society. And we must learn how to answer effectively society's insistence on accountability.

As a nation we must express our political will, to let our political leaders at all levels know that education is an issue of national security. If our united voice is clear, they will respond. We must be careful not to confuse our disagreement over the specifics of a particular proposal with the need to build a new system of education. We can all share in the prosperity—if we can learn to live together in harmony, as one of the leaders in the world community of nations. We have the national resources to experiment with new models, to try alternatives, to recover quickly from our mistakes, and ultimately to achieve the best possible national defense: the enlightened productivity of all Americans.

You can help us begin.

Acknowledgements

Many persons contributed to this book through discussion, reflection, and feedback and helped us shape our proposals on the specific issues we raise. The effort took more than three years and went through a dozen drafts

Bill's wife, Dr. Camille Cosby, has long urged attention to the issues we discuss. Dwight's wife, Dr. Carole Allen, and his son Dr. Douglas Allen, Associate Professor of Human Resources Management at the University of Denver, were constant reviewers of successive drafts. Patrick O'Shea was our principal research assistant. Charles Kipps was a valued source of support, offering a noneducator's viewpoint and seasoned editorial perspectives. Americom Research provided us with survey data from Internet users responding to our issues to help us factor in popular views of the relative importance of our proposals.

You, the readers, need to thank Jessica Papin, our Time Warner editor, who put it all together in the end, suggesting alternatives for numerous examples of "education speak" and was an effective advocate for you, seeking answers in advance to questions our readers might ask.

Others whose help we much appreciate include Mandy Allen, Dale Baird, David Berliner, Maurice Berube, Rebecca Bowers, Bob Brinton, Sarah Cella, Cathy Cheely, Phil Christensen, Jim Cooper, Danny Curry-Corocran, Tasha Curry-Corcoran, Chris Daggett, Lindsey Dame, Chris Dede,

Scott Field, Chris Fischer, Tim Fisher, Brian Fountain, Bill Geisler, Chris Giersch, Jane Hager, Kurt Hein, Walter Heinecke, Katurah Hein, Dan Hicks, Jonathan Higgins, Nancy Kaminski, David Kemp, Jennifer Kemp, John Khadem, Greg Kintz, Alyce Le Blanc, Han Liu, Krister Lowe, Robert Lucking, Lisa Madrey, Neal McBride, Sharon Margolis, Ruth Martin, Mike Melnik, Kelly Molini, James Onderdonk, Brett Parent, Aaron Popp, Simon Richmond, Kevin Ryan, William Smith, Tim Taylor, Thane Terrill, Clay Thorpe, Duane Varan, Lee Vartanian, Weiping Wang, Timothy Wirth, Denny Wolfe, Steve Zaloudek, and Ora Zohar.

—Dwight Allen and William H. Cosby, Jr.

Proceeds from the sales of this book will support the Dwight and Carole Allen Foundation, to be used for educational reform.

To make a contribution to the Dwight and Carole Allen Foundation to support educational reform, please visit our Web site at dcallenfoundation.org

If you are interested in helping out, let us know.

Visit our Web site at
americanschools100b.com

Register your opinions about our
18 specific proposals at
www.research.net/allen-cosby

Contact Dwight Allen and
William H. Cosby, Jr. by e-mail at
allen-cosby@mindspring.com

Printed in the United States
78421LV00002B/106-153